# Laughing Buddha:

## The Alchemy of Euphoric Living

by

**Sakshi Chetana**

I L P

Inner Light Publishers

www.inner-light-in.com

*Published by:*

INNER LIGHT PUBLISHERS

www.inner-light-in.com

ISBN: 9788191026948

E-mail: innerlight.in@gmail.com

*To the real Laughing Buddha,*
*who lives within us all*

# Contents

# Preface

In my experience and experiment with Buddhism as a way of life, I have often felt the need for a manual that could directly provide one the simple insights for happy living. For long, I was in search for a means to fill in the gap, the gap between the philosophy and the practices for joyful living. This is exactly where the Laughing Buddha came and fit in. Laughing Buddha is highly regarded as a storehouse of positive energy and an emblem of happiness and good luck. But I have found more in it than just a Feng-Shui remedy for problems. I have found the alchemy of euphoric living embedded in and personified by this extraordinary epitome of happiness. I have written this book because I want to share with you some simple insights and practices that you can begin to use right away and benefit from them, no matter what situation you are in, or what religious faith you happen to share. This book provides a simple manual to help you live a happier, more meaningful and fulfilling life for leading a euphoric life in the midst of the everyday work and responsibilities.

The Laughing Buddha indeed shows us that it is possible for all of us to live a radiant life like a living laughing Buddha. This book provides simple, easy to use recipe for euphoric living, following simple Buddha insights and keeping the jolly demeanor of the Laughing Buddha in front of us. In preparing this book, I have consciously tried to abstain from using Buddhist terms that might add any religious flavor to the book. Instead, I have tried to make it a simple manual to be used by any common person with little or no understanding of any religion or Buddhism. In preparing this book, I have been helped by many of my friends. I am deeply grateful to all of them.

Sakshi Chetana

# Chapter One

## Laughing Buddha: The Facts and Legends

In many utility stores or malls around the world, you will find his statues. The Laughing Buddha is now a dominant feature of the Chinese Buddhist and Shinto culture, though it has widely spread in many other countries and is adored as a symbol of fortune and happiness. The Laughing Buddha's statues grace many temples, restaurants, and ornaments in many traditions. He is regarded as an incarnation of the bodhisattva Maitreya who is supposed to appear as the Future Buddha. A bodhisattva is one who takes the vow to dedicate his or her life and spiritual practices for the good of all sentient beings in heaven and earth. The Laughing Buddha is extremely popular In China, where he is also known as the Loving One or the Friendly One. He is derived from an unusual Chinese Zen monk who lived well over a thousand years ago. He inspired the ordinary people to live their life more joyfully, mindfully and gracefully.

## Laughing Buddha and the Historical Buddha

The laughing Buddha is different from the historic Gautama the Buddha. However, he lived the essential spirit taught by the Buddha and also, is believed to be an incarnation of the Buddha. The historical

Buddha (Siddhartha Gautama) was born in Nepal. He came to India in search for enlightenment. After six years of seeking, learning and moving from one master to another in India, in search for the ultimate meaning of life, he reached Bodh Gaya in India. Under a Pipal tree on the bank of the river Niranjana at Bodh Gaya, he discovered the meaning of life and the way to release from the suffering of life. He attained his final enlightenment under the full moon of a starry night in the month of May at the age of thirty-five in the year 528 BC. His teachings consisted of what he called 'The Noble Eightfold Path' to go beyond sorrow. His teachings and philosophies came to be known as 'Buddhism'. Buddhism is not learning about a bunch of strange beliefs from a faraway land from someone who lived long ago. Buddhism is really a way of life. It is about looking at and thinking about our own lives. It shows how to understand ourselves and how to cope with our daily problems to actually be able to live a joyful life.

However, unlike many organized religions, where their founders are worshiped, in the Buddhist tradition, "the Buddha" is only highly regarded and admired as a great teacher. He is not seen as the savior. He is usually considered as an enlightened person who is able to help people, show them the way out of their suffering and teach about the nature of life and universe.

In the eastern traditions, such as the ones prevailing in India, China, Japan, Nepal and Tibet, any person who has been spiritually enlightened is called a Buddha. The Buddhist religion recognizes the appearances of many such 'enlightened ones' over the centuries. The Laughing Buddha is believed to be one such incarnation.

## The History of Laughing Buddha

Over a thousand years ago, there was a Zen monk who lived in a small province in China. His name was Quieci. He was affectionately called

Ch'i-t'zu. Ch'i-t'zu was an eccentric but loved character who worked small wonders such as predicting the weather. He lived presumably around the eighth century. Some say that he lived in China during the Later Liang Dynasty (907- 923 CE). He was a native of Fenghua. He was considered a man of good and loving character.

This monk was extraordinary in that he did not bear the usual somber air of the monks or religious persons. He was very jolly, helpful, compassionate and almost always in a mood of joyful celebration of life. He was always found laughing; hence the name the Laughing Buddha. He taught people to live life happily, enjoying the simple moments of joys that the life brings. People loved and admired this joyful, almost always euphoric character. People used to call him "Budhai", the word being derived from the "Buddha", meaning the enlightened one. In course of time, after his death, people forgot his original name, though they could not forget this simple, euphoric personality, who showed them the way to a joyful living. They used to remember him by the name "Budhai". The story of the laughing Buddha "Budhai" spread across many countries in the Asia, including Japan and India. Budhai, in Japanese accent became "Ho-tai". In many other accents he became Hotei or Pu-Tai.

After his death the laughing Buddha was proclaimed to be the re-incarnation of Siddhartha Gautama, the historical Buddha. Some Buddhist traditions consider him a Buddha or a bodhisattva, often identifying him as an incarnation of Maitreya, the future Buddha. Maitreya is named in the Tripitaka as the Buddha of a future age. His identification with the Maitreya Buddha is attributed to a Buddhist hymn, which was attributed to him. He is said to utter the following lines before his death:

"Maitreya, the true Maitreya
has billions of incarnations.
Often he is manifested from time to time;
But people seldom recognize him."

Statues of Budhai or Budai form a central part of I Kuan Tao shrines, where he is usually referred to by the Sanskrit name Maitreya. According to I Kuan Tao, he represents many teachings, including contentment, generosity, wisdom and open kindheartedness. He is said to help people realize their true essence within, which connects them with all beings. Pu-tai or Hotei followed the spread of Buddhism into other parts of Asia. In Japanese folklore, Hotei came to be regarded as one of the seven lucky gods of Taoism.

## The Statues of Laughing Buddha

The Laughing Buddha statues are usually represented by a laughing, fat and bald man in monk's robes, with an exposed pot-bellied stomach, symbolizing happiness, good luck, and good fortune. Some statues also have small children at his feet. Laughing Buddha statues often have an alms bowl in one of his hands representing his Buddha nature. Some Laughing Buddha statues are depicted as wearing or carrying prayer beads. He is often pictured as entertaining or being entertained by adoring children. His figure appears as a symbol of supreme contentment.

Some statues of the Laughing Buddha are seen carrying a linen sack, which is always full, signifying abundance and good luck. The sack is usually full with many valuable items, such as the rice plants, indicating wealth, sweets for children, and other food items for the poor and the needy.

In some other statues, the Laughing Buddha may be found on a cart drawn by children, or holding a fan called an Oogi. All of these features represent the Laughing Buddha as an itinerant monk who travelled and helped people on his way, taking away the burden of sadness from the people of the world.

The Chinese Legend has it that if you rub the Laughing Buddha's large stomach lovingly, it will produce wealth, good luck, and good fortune for you. The custom is strange, but heart-touching, nevertheless. The man who knows to laugh in every situation that life may pose, needs nothing from you but your heartfelt love; this must be the message.

## Laughing Buddha Statues in China

There are four Buddhist temples in Taiwan, which have the Laughing Buddha as their main Buddha statues. The Treasure Cognition temple in Taichung has Taiwan's tallest Laughing Buddha statue with his bald head touching the ceiling of the main temple hall. The Lingyin Temple in Hangzhou province of China has the biggest Laughing Buddha in China. It is carved from camphor wood and stands over 60 feet tall, and is gilded with over one hundred ounces of gold leaf.

## Laughing Buddha in Feng-Shui

The Laughing Buddha is one of the most popular symbols used by Feng Shui, the Chinese art of design and placement of objects. According to Feng-Shui, if the objects are placed correctly they are able to bring harmony and prosperity in our lives. Laughing Buddha has been the ultimate symbol of happiness, abundance and fortune in Feng Shui. He is often given the status of a deity. It is believed that he takes away all our problems, worries and stress. He helps us to overcome sadness and obstacles and offers a smooth life filled with happiness. Keeping this figurine at the place of business is said to enhance business and wealth.

Many believe that the Laughing Buddha absorbs negative Chi energy and emanates positive energies. A good Laughing Buddha image for Feng-Shui should have a smiling expression to signify fulfillment and joy.

The Laughing Buddha statues or idols are often found with symbols of wealth and abundance, such as pots of gold or a bag of treasure. Legend has it that the Laughing Buddha always carried in his bag candy for the children and foods and other necessities to help the poor. His statues always portray him having a fat belly, which is thought to be a symbol of happiness, good luck, wealth and generosity. The big belly of the Laughing Buddha is believed to hold deeper laughter, and it can stomach all your troubles and transmute them into happiness.

His large elongated earlobes are a sign of wisdom. His prayer mala is imprinted with a symbol that means good fortune. Happiness is one of his most treasured gifts. Many people believe that the Laughing Buddha can grant all your wishes, if you massage his belly 50 times and ask him to grant your wish. The Feng-Shui places great importance in his power to bring good luck in family and business.

Depending on the nature of the requirement, Feng-Shui recommends several types Laughing Buddha statues. If money and wealth energy is needed, then Feng-Shui recommends a statue of Laughing Buddha with gold ingots, which should be placed in the southeast corner of the home. For health and healing, Feng-Shui advises to keep the Laughing Buddha statue in the eastern zone of the home. The Laughing Buddha icons come with a variety of postures and possessions to be used as Feng-Shui remedies to many problems of life. Some of them are as follows:

## Laughing Buddha for Good Relationship

The Laughing Buddha statues sitting in a relaxed manner, with his eyes filled with love and compassion, are considered auspicious for building good relationship and nurturing happy family life.

## Laughing Buddha for Wealth and Prosperity

The Laughing Buddha statues holding a pot of gold or a bag filled with gold nuggets are believed to bring good finance and are considered very auspicious to be placed in an office or business. There is also a Laughing Buddha statue available, which is sitting on a toad carrying a gold coin in its mouth. This one too is an obvious prescription for bringing monetary abundance.

## Laughing Buddha for Receiving Abundance and Good Luck

Such a statue of the Laughing Buddha is seen to hold a bowl up to the Universe for receiving abundance and good fortune. It is believed to bring overall good luck.

## Laughing Buddha for Safe Travel

Laughing Buddha statues are often seen travelling on a cart carrying a hemp sack. This statue is considered auspicious for safe travelling and protection.

## Laughing Buddha for Happy Home

Laughing Buddha statues are often found sitting on large gold nuggets, which represent solid foundation. Such statues are considered good for creating a happy home.

## Laughing Buddha for Spiritual Wisdom

Laughing Buddha statues are sometimes dressed in fine robes, with a fan in one hand, symbolizing understanding, and a sack on the other, symbolizing gathering of insights. Such statues are believed to bring spiritual wisdom.

## Laughing Buddha for Long Life

The Laughing Buddha statues are sometimes found sitting with a large hat, as if enjoying the life in a care-free manner. Such statues are believed to bestow a problem-free long life.

## Placements of the Laughing Buddha Statue: Feng-Shui rules

Feng-Shui also has specific instruction for proper placements of the Laughing Buddha statue in a home or business. The living room or a table at the opposite to the main door of your work-place is generally considered as the best place to put the Laughing Buddha statues. Feng-Shui recommends placing it in such a place that it would welcome all the guests and prosperity that may enter the main door. Alternatively, the statue can also be placed in the wealth (south-east), health (east) or relationship (south-west) corner to increase the positive energy of the respective area. Feng-Shui recommends treating your Laughing Buddha statue with respect and it should not be placed on the floor. It is also not advised to place your Laughing Buddha icon in the bathroom or the bedroom.

Another important aspect most emphasized in a Feng-Shui remedy is maintaining the cleanliness of the statue. Keeping the Laughing Buddha clean and shiny is very important for attracting positive vibrations. Cleaning the Laughing Buddha Statue often with salt-water and placing it in the rays of the Sun in the early morning are advised as ways to enhance and maintain the effectiveness of the statue. And the most important part of it is making some positive intentions and asking for what you want, while being in a receptive mood.

Laughing Buddha has immense importance in Feng-shui. However, it is not just a Feng-Shui ornament or icon to be kept at one corner of your home for happiness. There is no doubt that Laughing Buddha statues emit vibrations of very high frequency and they have an important place in the Feng-Shui for bringing happiness, peace and prosperity. However, they can do much more than that. They can be used to teach and remind us of the way of living a mindful, alert and happy life, which is the true Buddha way of living.

The Laughing Buddha statues or icons remind us that a happy life is indeed attainable in this world and it comes with self-mastery, cultivating a happy demeanor, engaging in purposeful endeavor and bearing a deep commitment to the welfare of others. All this awaken the enlightened awareness within us, enabling us to live like a Laughing Buddha.

## Zen Philosophy, Laughing Buddha and Stories

After the Buddha attained enlightenment, his teachings spread far and near in the southwest Asia. Buddhist meditation became popular among the monks and laities. In Sanskrit, meditation is called Dhyan. Dhyan became Chan in Chinese accent and Zen in Japanese accent. Zen began to emerge as a distinctive school of Mahayana Buddhism when the Indian sage Bodhidharma (ca. 470-543) visited China and taught at the Shaolin Monastery of China. To this day, Bodhidharma is called the First Patriarch of Zen. The Zen tradition is a tradition of meditation as a way of life. With the passage of time, Zen assumed a distinct flavor of its own. Whatever we do in our ordinary life, can be done in the spirit of Zen. This is the core teaching. Eating, drinking, walking, everything done in this spirit can be divine. Zen does not draw a line between the sacred and the secular.

The laughing Buddha, Budhai is regarded by many as a Zen master. The primary story that associates Budhai in Zen (Chán) is a short Koan or mystical poem of the Zen tradition. It says that Budhai was travelling and giving candy to poor children. He used to ask only a penny from Zen monks or laities, those whom he met on his way. One day a monk walks up to him and asks, "What is the meaning of Zen?" Budhai looked at him, winked and dropped his bag, without saying anything. It indicated that Zen means being silent and dropping or letting go of all the baggages, which symbolize the burdens of thoughts, worries and anxieties. The monk asked again "How does one realize Zen?" At this, Budhai took up his bag and silently continued on his way. This symbolizes that Zen is realized by being silent and mindful right in the midst of the duties of our ordinary life.

Budhai is associated with the last image of a series of ten spiritual Masters. These are ten images that represent stages of enlightenment in Ch'an (Zen) Buddhism. The last image shows an enlightened master who enters towns and marketplaces to give the ordinary people the blessings of enlightenment.

The wonderful character of the Laughing Buddha as if poses a challenge to the boredom and pains of ordinary life. Suffering is ingrained in the very nature of life; this is one of the basic tenets of Buddhism. Old age is suffering; disease is suffering; death is a suffering, among other minor afflictions. How can anybody maintain a laughing gesture, an authentic jovial mood continuously amidst all these afflictions? As we have a glimpse of our Buddha nature, when we truly realize the interconnectedness of all that is, we can be authentically happy. But we do not have to wait for that. Being happy is more a state of mind than an outer condition. There are some wonderful Zen stories with central characters that mimic the state of the Laughing Buddha.

One such story goes like this. There was a Zen Master who seemed to be joyful, always. People have never seen him grumbling or unhappy. Once, one of his disciples asked him, "Master, what is the secret of your happiness?" The Master soberly looked at the disciple and winked. "Nothing special. It can be anybody's secret", he said; "Listen; I used to be like you people at my youth. Sometimes I was joyful; sometimes I was unhappy. Unhappiness used to come suddenly from nowhere. One day I examined my feelings and found that it really feels good to be happy and it hurts to become unhappy. That very day I decided that I want to be happy, no matter what comes. From that day I am living like this and I have never allowed unhappiness to take me over. It is as simple as this."

There is another such story. There was a Zen Master who used to make fun of everything. He was always found in a jovial mood. He did not allow anybody to be in a somber mood in front of him. He was getting old and his body became fragile. Still, he was as jovial as ever. When he was on his deathbed, one of his disciples said "Master, your presence is so precious to us. People will definitely cry when you pass away." "No." Said the Master. "I'll surely not allow anybody to do that. There will be smile in the face of all of you even when I die." The disciples were intrigued at this strange prediction of their Master. However, one day the inevitable happened. The Master passed away. There were tears in the eyes of everybody. How could they not miss such a wonderful person? However when his body was cremated, strange sounds began to emanate from that. The sounds of fireworks! He had somebody to secretly tie them all over his robes. The disciples began to smile even in the midst of their sorrow. Such a Master definitely deserves a smiling farewell, they thought in a heart, full of amazement, love and gratitude.

In these stories, the teachers, though seems somewhat unusual or eccentric from the judgment of the ordinary minds, they are really known as Buddhas or great teachers of life. Life should be lived in a spirit of celebration, they taught. The characters of these stories may be purely metaphorical, having little or no relation with the original Laughing Buddha. Still the similarity of the spirit is noticeable. In Thailand, Budhai is sometimes confused with another similar monk widely respected in Thailand. His name is Phra Sangkajai or Sangkachai. Phra Sangkajai, was a Buddhist Arhant or enlightened master. Arhant or Arhat (in Sanskrit) means one who have conquered and gone beyond all the mental defilements.

It is said that even the Lord Buddha praised Phra Sangkadchai for his excellence in explaining sophisticated Dharma in an easily and comprehensible manner. One tale relates that he was so handsome that once even a man admired him and wanted him for a wife. To avoid such situations, Phra Sangkadchai decided to transform himself into a fat monk. Another tale says that he was so beautiful that angels and men often compared him with the Buddha, which he considered inappropriate. Hence, he disguised himself in an obese body.

Although both Budhai and Phra Sangkajai may be found in both Thai and Chinese temples, Phra Sangkajai is found more often in Thai temples and adored as Budhai is adored in China. However they may not be the same persons.

# Chapter Two

## The Way of the Buddha and Euphoric Living

Think positively. Take responsibility of your life. Light up the flame of self-awareness. This was the essence of the teachings of all the Buddhas manifested through countless eons. Though the teachings of Buddhism are classified under the name of a single person known as the 'Buddha', these teachings are of universal nature and they were taught by all the enlightened ones of all ages in the history of humankind. Buddhism teaches that there is a body of universal Law (which the Buddha called the 'Dharma' or 'Dhamma', in Pali) that underlies everything in this universe. This is the core essence of life. You can also think of it as the basic rhythm of life and the Universe. To practice Buddhism is to bring our individual life in harmony with this greater principle of life of the universe. Making your life aligned to this universal rhythm of existence will enable you to experience greater wisdom and courage, more vitality and compassion, which are the fundamental qualities of this life-essence.

Euphoria is the gift of a healthy, balanced and energetic life. Everybody wants to feel contentment, happiness, and love. Nobody wants stress, pain, fear, rejection, and failure. The Buddha's teachings chart out a way to attain a healthy, balanced and happy life. It has nothing to do with religion, but has everything to do with your lifestyle. Though Buddha is widely regarded as a great religious figure, he actually was a very down-to-earth man who found out the way to a happy living and handed down the formula for the future generations.

As discussed earlier, the Buddhist religion recognizes the appearances of many 'enlightened ones'. The Laughing Buddha is believed to be one such enlightened master. After the spread of Siddhartha Gautama's teachings to China, the religion there had become too sanctimonious and somber. The Laughing Buddha brings in the Zen spirit of living life joyfully and zestfully, adding divine flavor to every aspect of the mundane life. The jolly, laughing figure of the laughing Buddha represents living life more fully and truthfully, in touch with the world and celebrating the extraordinary nature of the ordinary life.

Though the basic tenet of Buddhism emphasizes much on sorrow, or "Duhkkha", in Pali or Sanskrit, the Laughing Buddha shows us that the focus is often placed on a wrong point by the Buddhist scholars and teachers. Sorrow can not be the focus of life, if one intends to live life fully. It is often due to this wrong emphasis that many people abhor Buddhism as a doctrine of escapism from life. It can not be denied that there is sorrow in life, just as there are many simple joyful moments in life. No life is an exception. Buddha way of living is a mindful way of living that teaches us to remain balanced and skillfully transcend the unhappy moments of life.

Living in this way, our inner wisdom blossoms and we are able to replace anxiety with calm. As we learn to quiet our mind, let go of self-defeating thoughts and images, and remain balanced in all situations, we are able to see beauty and grace in all of life as we reach new heights of awareness. We begin to feel a remarkable sense of oneness with this entire planet and a profound feeling of peace and trust pervades our mind. This creates remarkable improvements in our mental, emotional and also physical health. We discover the true purpose of our life and our life is empowered with a joyful and powerful intention of living life more deeply, instead of just floating on the surface, barely managing to make the ends meet. This shift in our attitude unleashes a natural healing energy within, which causes a natural euphoric state of mind.

## Thinking positively

Does the Laughing Buddha show us the Buddha way of living, which is another name for living joyfully? Surely he does. The Buddha said, "We are shaped by our thoughts; we become what we think. When the mind is pure, joy follows like a shadow that never leaves". The statue of the laughing Buddha reminds us just that. What did he mean by a pure mind? A pure mind is that state of mind which is free from the contamination of negative thoughts and afflictions. How can the mind become pure? By practice, of course. The way is clearly laid down by the Buddha. Right meditation and right thinking are two of these royal ways shown by the Buddha himself. We need to cultivate positive thinking. We need to surround ourselves with positive, optimistic and energetic people. Then everything works out and our life becomes great. Fear, anger, hatred and worry create negative energy within us that destroy our lives. Learning to be mindful about our thoughts and emotions are vital for our well being. We need to be vigilant so that those destructive emotions can not enter our lives.

Buddha's way is really very simple. Here we do not want to go in to the scholarly details of the Buddhist philosophy (there are plenty of books available for that). His one teaching is sufficient to realize the whole gamut of the Buddhist doctrine. "Mind is the forerunner of all thoughts." He said. What does that have to do with my happiness? You might wonder. Everything; the Buddha would say. Much unhappiness in our lives follows from the thoughts in our mind. Mind is a creative entity. Our thoughts can create happiness and unhappiness, both for us. Beside that, happiness is a state of mind; not an object. Hence, if you watch over your mind and make the diligent and consistent practice of thinking positively always, happiness will surely follow. The statue of the Laughing Buddha can act as a good friend in this regard. Whenever we are off the track, his smiling face can bring us back to the present moment, to a positive mood. It is often impossible to maintain a grumpy attitude in front of a laughing friend.

You can put the statue of the Laughing Buddha at such a place in your home that may remind you to smile and laugh wholeheartedly at least once a day. Learning to laugh and giggle at small wonders of life will raise your vibration to much higher level. The next time you look at a statue or picture of a Laughing Buddha at your home do not just move on unmindfully, with your head crowded with thousands of thoughts. Just use the statue as a reminder to stop for a moment, breathe deeply and smile, before you go on your way. This simple practice will bring much happiness and light to your life.

When you think positively and laugh wholeheartedly, you are aligned with the universal law of life. When you are aligned with the universal law of existence, it enables you to laugh and smile more from your heart. The Laughing Buddha can be a reminder to bring your individual life into harmony with the greater principle of life of the universe.

We do not need to be a 'Buddhist' to keep the statue of the Laughing Buddha in our homes. Similarly, we do not need to be initiated to any organization to follow the simple teachings of the Buddha which can make our lives more joyful and harmonious. The Laughing Buddha can remind us to live with greater wisdom and courage, to live with more vitality and compassion. This is what it means to live and manifest the conditions for an enlightened life. A smile or laugh can lighten up your day like a ray of the Sun, thus warding off all negative thoughts.

## Taking the responsibility

Thus the way of the Buddha begins by taking responsibility of our lives. Nobody but we ourselves are responsible for our life, health and happiness. Nobody but we ourselves are responsible for the way we think, the things we believe and the thoughts we entertain. When you acknowledge that, you begin to take the responsibility of your thoughts. As you begin to take the responsibility of your thoughts, you begin to realize that you are the creator of your reality, because our thoughts create our reality.

It is in human nature to shift the responsibility on anyone but themselves; we do not like to own up. We try to transfer the blame on anything or anyone; may it be fate, family, society, nature or parents. The moment we gather enough courage to bring the focus on ourselves, and look within, a new dimension is added to our life, and we are on the royal road to transformation, transformation from unconscious pattern of boredom, pain and suffering to the freedom of conscious choice and happiness. We can do this right here in the middle of our everyday life.

The technique, Buddha offered us for this, is called mindfulness or aware observation. We neither blame, nor condemn ourselves. We just own up. We just open up to ourselves. Thus comes the right understanding. Thus comes the right thinking. Thus come the right action and right concentration. Everything else follows. The Buddha never claimed himself to be anybody other than an ordinary human being. No inspiration, no message, no powerful transmission from any superior being or God was claimed by Siddhartha Gautama, when he attained enlightenment. He attributed his awakening to intelligent and sincere effort, which may be the prerogative of every human being. We need to exert effort to be mindful of our thoughts, attitudes and beliefs.

## Cultivating right attitude

The idol of laughing Buddha is an epitome of right attitude. Our attitude and thoughts are most important for our happiness. We need to appreciate our mind, our body, our life, our planet and this grand Universe. Recent discoveries in quantum physics have changed the conventional way of thinking. Scientists have acknowledged that we are part of the world we view and hence, the observer participates in any event by the very process of his or her observation. Accordingly, the process of our observation changes the things we observe. It is true for an electron, as it is true for an event or a person in our lives.

Eastern mystics had known this principle long before. Our attitude determines how we look at a thing, a person or an event. Hence our attitude is the main ingredient that determines the chemistry of our experience as a human being. Negative attitudes to life, persons and events are harmful, as they conjure up negative situations in our experience. Just the same way a positive attitude to life, event and people can present us with positive or pleasant experiences and situations.

Our beliefs are also important. We need to closely examine our beliefs. We shape our world through our belief. All we speak, act and do is shaped and guided by our belief. Our interactions with the others are shaped and guided by our belief. We pick up our beliefs from various sources in the process we grow up. People injure themselves by the negative ideas and beliefs they entertain. Nobody was born with negative attitudes. In our unawareness, negative ideas and beliefs enter us from external situations, persons we trust, friends, relatives, media, existing beliefs of the society and the culture we live in. The negative ideas and beliefs, when entertained, block the flow of Grace within us. Diseases in the body and conflicts outside grow as a result. Positive beliefs unlock the healing potential within us. We should consciously practice love, trust, appreciation, happiness, satisfaction, patience, peace, and gratitude in our everyday life.

## Lighting up the flame of self-awareness

*"Therefore, Ananda, be a lamp unto yourself, be a refuge to yourself. Take help of no external refuge. Hold fast to the Truth as a lamp; hold fast to the Truth as a refuge. Look not for a refuge in anyone beside yourself. And those, Ananda, who either now or after I am dead shall be a lamp unto themselves, who take themselves to no external refuge, but holding fast to the Truth as their lamp, and holding fast to the Truth as their refuge, shall not look for refuge to anyone beside themselves, it is they who shall reach the highest goal."* --- Buddha (Mahaparinibbana Sutta)

**"Be a light unto yourself and take refuge within yourself"**, this was the essential message of the Buddha. There is this light within all of us. We live by this light; we breathe by it and have our beings within it. It is inside of our beings and also outside. We are nourished and sustained by it. All sentient beings carry this light within them, though unaware of it. Only we, the human beings are endowed with a nervous system so wonderful and sophisticated that we are capable of being aware of this light and by being aware of this light, we become the light; our earthly being is illumined by this light. This light is the light of self-awareness.

In this process of self awareness, we learn to be aware of our bodily postures and gestures, of our feelings, sensations, of our breath and of our thoughts and emotions. As a human being, we possess a body that can stand upright and a mind that thinks. We can do much with these two wonderful instruments. The soul is beyond our ordinary level of perception. Hence the Buddha never mentions that in any of his teachings.

According to the Buddha, our self-awareness begins with the awareness of our body, its postures and the ordinary sensations it produces. Following his teachings, we learn to bring our attention back and forth through the body, from head to feet and feet to head, all the while remaining in a state of equanimity. We learn to simply observe and experience things for what they are, without trying to change anything, without trying to repress the unpleasant sensations and without craving for the pleasant sensations.

The Buddha taught that sensations in the body are the doorways to the deeper layers of the mind. Energy follows attention. So, as we bring our awareness into our body, its energy pattern and resonance begins to change. Over the time we discover that what we have previously experienced as gross matter is teeming with subatomic currents of light.

In the next level, we learn to become mindful of our thoughts and emotions right in the midst of our everyday life. We learn to observe things objectively without being entangled by judgment or labeling.

This process of self awareness is also called the art of witnessing. Witnessing is the way of the seers, the way of all the Buddhas. When you are able to watch yourself, you will be able to know yourself. When you know yourself, you will go beyond the land of sorrow. It is said that, by observing others you become wise, and by observing yourself you become enlightened. This was the message of the Buddha. This was the message of Lao Tzu. The saying, "Know thyself," was also written on the temple of the oracle at Delphi in ancient Greece. You need to understand yourself on all levels.

Are you thinking that it is easier said than done? True; you need patience, persistence and, above all, a rock-solid intention to do it, in the beginning. However, the reward is so vast and magnificent that in the long run you will be happy that you tried it. It doesn't matter how much successful you are, in doing it; it doesn't matter how much or how little you are able to do this. It is understandable that at the beginning your attention will stray from your body; you will obviously be entangled in your thoughts instead of observing them. However if you just succeed in being persistent in the effort to observe yourself, within a short while, you will notice that you have grown a knack of it. You will begin to love this process of being aware of yourself on all levels. Really, self-awareness is another name of self-love.

Slowly you will be able to discover the automatic patterns of your behavior. The reasons behind your fears or worries and many other secrets of the body and mind, hitherto unknown, will be revealed to you. The reason, why you act or react in a certain way in a certain situation, will be clear to you. You will be pleasantly surprised by the fact that by being aware of a negative thought or a psychological irritant, they disappear most of the time, or lose their power over you. If you continue with this process of self-observation, you will be surprised to notice, probably for the first time in your life, that almost in every situation, you have a choice as to how you may think, speak `or act. Every situation in life presents us with an array of choices. An alert person is aware of those choices. An unaware person is not.

When you learn to observe yourself, previously what used to be an automatic reaction, seemingly so obvious, now seems like a mere choice, which you are free to opt for or not. As you become more and more alert and aware, you become conscious of your choices. This is so much liberating. You are no longer dictated by the automatic mechanical impulses of the body and mind.

Suppose, someone says something unbecoming to you. It creates a painful sensation within you. That is very natural. Previously your automatic reaction to it would be striking back with some sharp comment. Now, that you are more alert, you are not in a hurry to strike back. You clearly see that, you have choices regarding your response to it. You have, as if eternity at your disposal to weigh the choices of your possible reaction, to peruse about the possible outcome of your response, or to see the motivation of the person behind saying so. Perhaps, you recognize her suffering, helplessness or worry that made her behave in that way. In any case, you are free to choose appropriate words of response that would convey your disappointment without engendering unconscious chain of negativity within you or without aggravating her suffering, especially if, she is a loved one.

There is a well-known anecdote related to the life of the Buddha. It goes like this. Once, the Buddha was out for begging. While he was passing through a certain village, a Brahmin, who was enraged upon him, approached him and began to slander him. Buddha sat their calmly, observing his breath, quietly waiting for the Brahmin to finish it all. After some time, the Brahmin came to his sense. He was stunned by the quiet forbearance of the Buddha. He asked the Buddha, how he could manage to maintain such a calm demeanor upon being insulted so much. The Buddha replied with a counter question. He asked, what the Brahmin was supposed to do if he visited a friend with some gift that the friend refused to accept. Obviously then, there would be nothing to do except taking the gift back with him, was the answer of the Brahmin. The Buddha replied with a smile that life has taught him to make the choice of not accepting certain gifts, the gifts such as those brought by the Brahmin.

If somebody wants to give you something undesirable, you have freedom of choice for not accepting it. If somebody says that, you are bad, it does not make you bad. You have the freedom of not accepting such a negative suggestion. You have the freedom to respond in a measured way without losing your clarity and composure.

Our self-awareness and observation take us to the deeper territory of our mind. We come to realize that, it is the mind which gives reality to any experience we might have. The same experience might have greater or lesser impact upon us depending upon the state of our mind at a certain moment. The same experience will have different impacts on two persons depending upon the state of their minds. Through self-study, the mind becomes mature, quiet and peaceful, which makes it fit for meditation. Witnessing makes you a master. Who is a master? A master is a person who is free from the slavery of the blind impulses of body and mind.

Thus way of the Buddha has the great potential to liberate us in the midst of our ordinary life. Self-awareness is another name of meditation. Self-awareness is another name of Zen. By practicing self-awareness, we learn to sit in Zen. We learn to walk in Zen. We laugh in Zen and we listen in Zen. Thus we can become living Laughing Buddhas.

## Wisdom in a Nutshell: The Buddha Way of Euphoric Living

1.  The way of the Buddha begins by taking responsibility of your life. Nobody but you are responsible for the way you think, the things you believe and the thoughts you entertain. By taking the responsibility of your thoughts, you begin to take responsibility of your life, health and happiness. As you begin to take the responsibility of your thoughts, you begin to realize that you are the creator of your reality.

2.  The next step is right thinking. As you realize the importance and impact of your thoughts, attitudes and beliefs on your life, you begin to cultivate and entertain only positive and wholesome thoughts and discard negative and unwholesome thoughts, beliefs and attitudes.

3. The second step highlights the need of cultivating self-awareness. In this process of self awareness, you learn to be aware of your bodily postures and gestures, of your feelings, sensations, thoughts and emotions. This gives you mastery over your mind.

# Chapter Three

## Living the Spirit of the Laughing Buddha

In spite of his obesity and apparently not so handsome appearance, he was, and till today is, loved and admired by people all over the world. In his lifetime he appeared to be eccentric to some people, because he was always found laughing or smiling. However, people could not help but love this wonderful 'eccentric' person. Can such a person really be called eccentric? If such a wonderful mental state of love, compassion and joy can be labeled as eccentricity, then such eccentricity is a blessing for the humankind. It is no small feat to always manage to be in a joyful mood. Even the eccentric or mad people have their blues. Actually mad or eccentric people fall below the mechanism called mind, as they are unable to use their mind; ordinary people are ruled by their unruly mind; whereas this little jovial fellow called Budhai or Hotei was able to transcend his mind; he was able to rule it in such a way that it was completely under his command. He could enjoy his life to the fullest.

What can we learn from the Laughing Buddha? We can learn to live our life in the spirit of the Laughing Buddha. He moved gracefully on this planet, dedicating most of his life to love and protect all beings, especially the children. He was a patron of the poor and weak. His very presence was a blessing to all. He knew how to relax and enjoy life to the fullest. He knew to love and laugh. The spirit of the Laughing Buddha can be summed up in two sentences: Love and laugh. Let go and relax.

## Love and Laugh

The laughing Buddha reminds us of the most important message from the Buddhist philosophy. You must have a loving heart to be happy. We are the waves of the same ocean. The Buddha taught that the whole existence is connected by an interdependent net of being. On each level of our existence, we are connected with, and dependent on, others. Even as the body and mind, our existence is dependent on other beings in the plant and animal kingdom. For example, the Sun is the source of our energy by which the physiological activities of our body run; but, the whole of the animal kingdom, including us, the human beings, are incapable of directly assimilating sunlight in our body. Only the plants are endowed with the capacity to store the energy of the Sun within their body through the process of photosynthesis. They are at the lowest end of the food chain from which the whole of the animal kingdom derives nutrition and the solar energy necessary for their survival.

Through food and water, we are connected to the earth. We, all of us, rich and poor, saint and sinner alike, breathe in the same air recycled by the plants. We are but tiny parts of an indivisible whole. Hence, by hurting others we cannot but hurt ourselves. By loving and helping others, we cannot but love and help ourselves. By sharing what we have with others, we are actually giving it back to ourselves. This law is ancient and infallible. So, not as a doctrine, dogma or maxim, but for our own good, we should embrace this ancient law of life.

This law is the law of loving and caring for others. This law is the law of giving and sharing with all the fellow beings on the planet. Love is the divine light that can melt away all inner blockages. Love heals our being at all levels. Modern medical science and psychology has also proved that love is a great healing force. Love and other such emotions that cause expansion of consciousness act as antidotes to the blockages created by hatred, anger, fear, anxiety, stinginess and other negative emotions. The negative emotions create resistances and secrete toxic chemicals, which are transformed, over the time, to subtle blockages in the neuromuscular systems that manifests as various physical and neurological ailments in the end. Love is the panacea for almost all diseases. Love heals the body, mind and nervous system. A loving heart spreads warmth and light. When you bear an attitude of love, caring and sharing, you feel relaxed and peaceful, and your inner light shines bright. Only when you feel light at heart you can laugh.

Laughter too is a great healing power like love. If you practice laughing or smiling often, although forcefully in the beginning, you will discover a strange phenomena. You will notice that suddenly the veil of gloom or boredom is evaporating to create a subtle lightness or happiness in your heart.

This has a deep scientific reason. An action or posture of the body conveys some signal to the mind and let the mind behave accordingly. If you try to act a sad character, you will find before long that you are really being sad and dejected for no obvious reason. Try to act angrily and anger will suddenly come from nowhere. The body can not distinguish between acting the role and the original thing. Thus it will secret chemicals and hormones to make your mind really angry and agitated. Just for the same reason, when you practice laughing and smiling, happiness will come. The body will take the signal to secrete hormones and chemicals to make you feel euphoric. Thus laughter can be a great tonic for a depressed mind.

A good belly laugh in the style of the laughing Buddha can light up your day, transcend all boundaries and melts away tension, stress, worry and conflicts. Try it yourself and see the result. You will be amazed. You will be able to relax more. You will be able to love yourself more. You yourself are just as deserving of your own love as is everybody in the world. Buddha taught tolerance and love, including self-love.

## Let go and relax

The statues of the Laughing Buddha teach us the ultimate relaxation. How could he be so relaxed? Like happiness, relaxation too is a mental phenomenon. You can not relax when you hold on to old grudges or anger. You can not relax when you become resentful. You can not relax when you feverishly hold on to a desired outcome. So, physical relaxation can do very little when you carry tensions inside you. If you are angry, if you are resentful, if you are resisting or rejecting something deeply, your muscles will carry those thoughts and emotions in the form of subtle tensions. If you want to really relax, you need to learn to take life less seriously. You need to learn to let go. Everything is impermanent in this life. This is the first noble truth taught by the Buddha. Remember it often. It will help you to let go and relax.

"Those who are free from resentful thoughts surely find peace", said the Buddha. We can follow his footsteps to be truly happy. So learning to let go is a must for being able to relax. Meditation can help you to relax too, because, meditation is nothing but a process, a technique for you to let go of your usual thoughts of worries, anxieties, fears or undesirable emotions that make you tense. Even physical relaxation can make you relax mentally to some extent.

One of the reasons that love is such a widely sought after emotion on earth, is because, of all worldly things it gives you the taste of ultimate relaxation. Though we have discussed these four faculties separately, these four faculties, love, laughter, letting go and relaxation are intertwined and interdependent. You can laugh only when you are truly, authentically happy. You can be truly happy when you love. You can love only when you know how to let go and relax. You can truly relax only when you practice letting go and you love. Thus you can begin by being more loving to discover that you can relax better and you laugh or smile more often. Or alternatively you can begin by meditating and learning relaxation only to find that you are being more loving and happy for absolutely no reason.

## The Spirit of Laughing Buddha: Buddha Wisdom in Nutshell

1. Being able to love and laugh from your heart sums up the core spirit of the Laughing Buddha. You must have a loving heart to be happy. You can laugh only when you are truly, authentically happy. You can be truly happy when you love, when you love and care for your fellow beings, when you give and share what you have. Find out reasons to laugh. A wholehearted laughter can relax you beyond measure. It has tremendous therapeutic value as well.

2. Letting go of grudges, anger and resentment is also very important for living the spirit of the Laughing Buddha. We feel light-hearted and free when we forgive and forget to move on with our life. Everything is impermanent, including our existence on this planet. Remembering this will help us to forgive and move forward. We can relax    physically and mentally, by cultivating an attitude of letting go, by taking life less seriously.

## Be a Beautiful Laughing Buddha

The idea of beauty varies from person to person, according to his or her social upbringing, taste and many other factors. However, we all agree that babies and children are beautiful. Irrespective of the nationality, caste or race it was born in to, the babies are beautiful. Why this is so? Babies are beautiful, because they live in a state of love, in a state of grace and oneness, without ever knowing what these concepts mean.

When we start living consciously and joyfully, with a genuine smile lingering on our lips, we become beautiful too. A genuine heartfelt smile can reflect an attitude of acceptance, gratitude and letting go. A heartfelt smile is born of an understanding and authentic heart which knows the meaning of love, freedom and interconnectedness of us all.

We become beautiful, irrespective of the color of our skin, or other characteristics of our physical being, when we learn to greet life with a smile. The Laughing Buddha, with his bald head and not-so-beautiful physical features, was definitely not the kind of person, to whom people would naturally feel attracted to. Still, the picture of his ecstatic countenance and laughter undoubtedly attracts many people all over the world. The reason for this is that he lived in total acceptance of his being. You become beautiful when you accept yourself completely and become courageous to be yourself, irrespective of what people think of you.

This happens when we take charge of our lives by tapping into our full potential to be an authentic and awakened human being. It will bring out the best version of who we really are. This happens when we remain aware of what is going on within and without. This happens when we are in perfect harmony with ourselves. The feeling of perfect balance and the sense of well-being radiates from within as a presence that is beautiful.

Every single day offers us the opportunity for a completely fresh beginning, a chance to start with a clean slate, with no baggage, no expectations, nothing holding us back. It is only our choice to start our life afresh, to live in an open and conscious way, creating joy and happiness for us and our fellow travelers in this journey, called life. Regardless of your situation, each breath you take can fill you with a new sense of freedom, with the possibility of a new beginning. The key is your choice. We all are born with the wonderful power of choice. We all have the choice to be beautiful, to live every moment like a Laughing Buddha, to free ourselves from the past, as fantastic or challenging as it might have been, and move forward into the next moment. Let the statue of the Laughing Buddha remind us to exert our choice to be beautiful.

# Chapter Four

## Practical Lessons: Living as Laughing Buddha

By now we know the basic principles for euphoric living. But still doubts peep in our mind. The laughing Buddha, and also the historical Buddha, we think, lived in a culture, which is so different from our cultural settings and nine to five work-a-day lives. Is it possible to maintain the smile under varied circumstances in our modern life? The Buddhas might be able to do so, but, for us, we know for sure that even if we sometimes experience the euphoric state of mind, particularly when everything goes right for us, this state is usually very short-lived, because, there are many situations in life which are not agreeable to say the least, and many psychological irritants exists hidden beneath the surface of the mind that do not allow us to live life to the fullest.

However there are some practical lessons of life which we need to know and apply in our daily lives for maintaining the smile on our lips. These practical lessons are ancient and time-tested and handed down to us by wise fellow human beings and Buddhas who knew how to maintain their balance against all odds. We will take up them in the following section.

## How to respond to an unpleasant situation?

When an external situation is perceived as psychologically unbalanced, it is often in our human nature to jump into the situation with all our energy, in an effort to fix or heal it. While we often do so, and it is understandable why we do so, this approach seldom helps, unless it is a tangible emergency like fighting a fire or so. With this attitude, we are much more likely to be drawn out of balance rather than re-establishing balance in the situation. In pouring all our energy into an unpleasant situation, what we often do is being off our center and completely exhausting ourselves.

Jumping in to a situation and being deeply involved in it often gets counter-productive in that our own energy often serves to feed the unpleasant situation instead of healing it. In fact, at such difficult times we should strive to maintain our own balance so that we spend less energy to feed the situation. We should be economical and wise in spending our energy. We can do that by being aware of maintaining our own balance. One sure way to seriously exhaust ourselves and cloud our clarity is attempting to take control of an unbalanced situation and wanting to force balance in to it on our own. This will not only drain us, but also aggravate the situation, because sometimes it is wise to allow a situation to resolve itself with additional time and adjustment. Trying to impose an immediate balance does not help.

Difficult situations usually trigger panic and breeds fear and other unwelcome emotions. While we should expect such human responses, and be understanding with them, we should be cautious not to give our energy behind it. We do so, not because we become indifferent or insensitive. On the contrary, we remain present with the situation, understand it correctly and take constructive steps while keeping our focus on maintaining our balance. We do so, because we understand that maintaining our own balance is a stronger force to heal the situation.

## How to live with an unpleasant situation?

We need to acknowledge that life does not always happen to us on our own terms. Unpleasant situations or circumstances may be there. We can not always change an unpleasant situation. However, if we approach life with awareness and understanding the unpleasantness will lose its sting. Sometimes it is beyond us to heal an unpleasant situation or remove ourselves from it. When a situation is perceived to be unpleasant, and can not be readily changed, what we need to do is try to understand the situation, learn our lessons from it, and live the situation by just being with it; all the while we need to be mindful to keep a balanced state of mind. Keeping our balance is of utmost importance.

Life is to be experienced in totality. It is possible if one makes the choice to live with greater awareness and understanding. Try not to blame others like spouse, parents, friends, fellow beings or situations for any suffering, because blaming does not help resolving a situation. You have to take charge of your own destiny by taking positive or corrective steps. Cultivating a positive state of mind under all circumstances is important. Never allow your vibe to go to a lower level. This way you will attract more and more positive circumstances in your life.

The quality of your life depends on how interested and intense you are in living it. Intensity of awareness unleashes the energy of wholesomeness. When you experience an unpleasant situation with full awareness, without thoughts of mental resistances, the sting of the situation dissolves and it becomes an empty phenomenon that is unable to disturb your mental poise.

## How to maintain our balance in every situation?

It is a decision you take, and you persistently be aware to implement it. Additionally, you might want to cultivate a higher level of energy within you that will help you to maintain your inner poise. For cultivating a higher energy state within you, it is necessary to take some moment everyday to become still and experience yourself. Stillness in itself is a higher energy state that establishes harmony within you and all around you. As you experience yourself in stillness, as you focus on your breath, sensation or your being, you will be able to experience the calm and quiet center within you that is free from all conflicts and turmoil. It is the centre within you that is free from the turmoil of thoughts.

This wonderful peace deep within you will change your notion about yourself. It is the truest and the most permanent thing about who you are. It is the divine essence of you. When you experience the peace and the still center within you, the quality of your life will change. Nothing will seem quite the same ever. You will no longer live your life from the surface of your mind which is often in turmoil stimulated by the external situations. You will be able to live your life from this still center. When you remember and feel this centre of stillness within you in every situation of life, you will feel more relaxed, restful, more sure about yourself and more enthusiastic in whatever you choose to do. You will have fewer worries, lesser fears and an abundance of life energy. You will know that all experiences are temporary and they are incapable of disturbing your original peace. Situations will continue, experiences will continue to be there, so long as we live; but they will be noted as nothing more than a passing film on the screen of life. Living in this way, life will be blissful.

## How to know what is right for you at a certain moment?

Try to watch your 'feel' at every moment. You will be in the right path. When you feel yourself deeply and allow the inner feeling to guide and direct your thoughts, words and actions, you can not go wrong. Pursue that which brings joy to you and which feels right. Honor your deepest feelings and live the life which you feel will bring you the feelings of fulfillment. It requires that you will be brave enough to follow your deepest impulses about what feels right. This is not always easy. It needs courage and trust on yourself.

## How to be free from guilt, shame or bad habits?

Feelings of guilt, shame, lack of confidence or bad habits do not allow us to become happy. They are inner enemies. How to be free from them? Self love and acceptance and self-observation are the keys. First learn to love and accept yourself, as you are; because, love is the only way to freedom and transcendence. Learn to love and accept your body, mind and being in its totality. Though this may sound obvious, there are very few who truly love themselves and act upon on their own interest. Loving yourself is the beginning of the journey to be free from guilt, shame, poor confidence or bad habits. The light of love is powerful beyond measure to heal all evils, including guilt, shame, poor confidence and bad habits.

People often say, "I do not love my look," or even worse, when someone says "I hate myself". This is a wrong approach to life. If you yourself are not able to love yourself, how can you expect anybody else in all the worlds to love you? When you begin to love and accept yourself, you become more beautiful, not because of any change in your physical features, but because of the light of self-love being radiated through your being. This light has the miraculous capacity to erase out all the imperfections of your character.

Accept yourself with all your strengths and faults, just as a loving mother accepts her child with care and concern. Even if the child is difficult, she accepts the child totally and still works for its improvement for its own good. Forgive yourself when you fail to live up to your expectation. It does not mean that you do not try to improve. You try to improve and you find it easier to make improvements and to drop out the undesirable traits, when you completely, lovingly accept yourself. But, admonishing yourself does not serve anything other than self-defeat and self-alienation. You can improve only when you have accepted yourself so totally that nothing is hidden in the backyard of your mind. Now you are able to watch those thoughts and feelings with certain detachment and you are free to take corrective steps. Know that every one of us is a unique creation of universal consciousness; consequently, all should have the freedom to be what they are, so long as they are not harming others.

## How to cope with fear born out of feeling of insecurity?

We can cope with fear and feeling of insecurity by learning to welcome changes. Feeling of insecurity is born of the mind's natural tendency to cling to the past. Mind likes to cling to the past, even when the past was not so good. Consequently, it resists any changes in the existing situation or circumstances. This is the reason why some people go on carrying the burden of a past relationship that has long been dead. We need to train our mind to accept and welcome the changes that come in our life. We should be in a positive frame of mind when changes knock at our door. Learning to welcome changes will make you brave and strong and all the fears of insecurity will drop away.

## How can we prepare ourselves to accept changes?

Change is an unalterable fact of this temporal existence. Change means end of something and beginning of another. Some changes in your life are welcomed by your mind, while some are not. When you learn to accept changes as an unalterable fact of life, you live at ease with life, gliding effortlessly through it, through the peaks of joys and the valleys of sorrows. Changes are the harbingers of a new beginning; changes give us the freedom to move forward by effortlessly shedding the past, like a snake sheds its old skin and never looks back.

As we have mentioned earlier, we, the human beings are often hooked in the habit of clinging to the existing situation or circumstances, be it good or bad. We do this because we like to be in our comfort zone. Changes make us feel insecure or uncomfortable. But changes are the only means that we can grow and improve. Welcoming changes means welcoming improvement and growth.

People like things to remain the same. In that, they even cling to their misery. If you do not embrace change, how can you hope to improve your life? Changes can be a harbinger for improvement in your life when you are conscious and optimistic. Even if the change happens to be of an unwelcome nature, like losing a job, or something like that, take it as a scope for betterment in life and not as a failure. Change is the heart of the process called life. Just look around and you will see that change is happening every day, every moment.

Changes are part and parcel of our lives. We change jobs; we change accommodations. New things, new friends, new persons enter our lives and existing ones depart. Sometimes these changes are something we take up voluntarily, sometimes they are involuntary. If the changes are voluntary, we are somewhat comfortable with them; if they are involuntary, we usually are uncomfortable with them and hence, we resist. Resistance brings pain. The loss of a loved one brings tremendous pain, because we resist it. When we can peacefully accept the change, we grow and the growth is beautiful. It does not inflict pain on us. We can prepare ourselves for accepting changes peacefully by acknowledging the impermanent nature of everything and believing that there is a higher purpose to everything that happens to us. Nature is wise beyond measure and universe is friendly to all of its creations. When we know and remember this, we become peaceful by accepting what it provides us for our growth.

We learn to be in good terms with change by practicing letting go. Letting go is the most important lesson that life can teach us. Consciously let go of everything that does not contribute to your sense of well-being. Letting go of the unnecessary burden of the past, letting go of the fixed ideas, letting go of the negative thoughts and emotions and accepting the changes that life brings, we become lighter and happier. By practicing letting go, the burden of life suddenly drops away and we can live and breathe a wonderful sense of freedom.

## Does living in the moment help?

It surely helps. Living in the moment means to flow with the time. As you flow with time, you spontaneously learn to embrace the change. Impermanence is the sacred law of Nature. Hence living in the moment, we follow the course of Nature. We adore and worship Nature by living in the moment. The reward is the feeling of deep happiness that naturally flows within us.

Getting rid of the excess baggage of the past makes life so much celebration, resulting in release and freedom. While it is important to take lessons from the past, we need not cling to the past. We should approach the life with a fresh outlook. Every day is a new beginning. Every moment is born fresh.

Living in this moment does not mean that you do not plan, or, you do not learn from your past mistakes. We should let our mind plan for the future; we let our mind train itself from the experiences it meets. However, we should not be trapped in the obsessive and unconstructive thoughts of past events or fantasies regarding the future.

See how you feel when you only focus on what is happening right now. As you continually do this, you will see yourself starting to enjoy the process. The obsessive, compulsive chatter of the mind lessens when you live in the moment. Thoughts will be fewer and fewer, until there is none and you will effortlessly feel the calm centre within you. You will be more and more blissful, as a result.

## Why observing the thoughts are important for happiness?

It might be difficult to believe, but our perception of the world is entirely constructed by our mind. Each person creates a personal reality of her own, which becomes a filter through which she experiences life. The mind has the power to create a world based on our most compelling and repetitive thoughts. When it comes to our external world, we normally remain very careful and watchful of the words and ideas we project, because we know for sure that the words or ideas we utter or write down have a definite consequence. But we pay little attention to our inner thoughts, because, we assume that the fleeting words, images and ideas that whirl through our heads are benign and they do not bear a consequence. This is wrong. Even our stray thoughts have huge impact on our lives.

Are you aware of negative thoughts you regularly entertain? Do you entertain thoughts such as 'I am useless', 'I can't do it', 'no-one likes me' or 'I have been cheated by life' etc.? If such thoughts or ideas are repeated, the mind will take them as true and make them your reality, even if you never say the words verbally. You will become a person who is really cheated, unloved or incompetent. The only way to change is to take command of your thoughts, either by observing them and carefully uprooting the negative self-dialogues or by conscious affirmation and practice of positive thoughts, ideas and emotions.

We will discuss more on this later. When we know that our thoughts create our destiny, we can not but take corrective steps to generate right thinking.

## How to tackle with strong negative thoughts and emotions?

Take a few deep breaths and breathe out the negative thoughts. In case of a strong upsurge of negative thoughts or emotions, just be aware of the sensations in your throat and check the sensations in your heart and abdomen. Feel where it feels most intense. As you breathe out take your attention there and imagine breathing out the negative emotion from that place. Continue to do so until the sensation reduces. For example, if it is felt most intensely in your heart area, continue to breathe out from the heart until you feel that the heaviness or numbness in your heart has softened or disappeared. Then again, breathe in and as you breathe out, check the centre that exists approximately two inches below the navel.

This technique is based on a wonderful secret discovered and taught by the Buddha. Every thought and emotion in our mind has a corresponding physical counterpart in our body, which manifest as a sensation; he used to teach. You might have noticed that your body becomes stiff when you experience anger. It is impossible for you to experience anger, if your body is hundred percent relaxed. Similarly your body shrinks when you experience hatred. Parts of your body become stiff, when you experience tension or anxiety.

Breathing in and out deeply relaxes your body and observing your breathing or sensation automatically relaxes your breath and deepens it; thus the body goes back to its original state of rest and relaxation soon as you take a few deep breaths. When all the sensations are gone, the thought and the feeling of hurt will disappear too. As you keep focusing your awareness on the sensations inside your body, the negative emotions disappear just as the clouds disappear in the presence of the Sun. You will be surprised to notice that, the knots and hurtful feelings born out of the negative emotions dissolve, as the sensations inside your body disappear.

This simple but powerful practice can prove extremely helpful at the time of distress when negative emotions like anger or fear ravages the mind. At times of urgency, when you do not have time to observe your breath or sensation, just take a deep breath and as you breathe out, feel that you release the negative emotion with the long outgoing breath. Repeat the process, with your attention focused on the outgoing breath. Within a short time, you will feel much relief. Be still in any moment of confusion, fear or anxiousness, and focus on your breath. In the stillness come the relaxation, clarity and solution.

## How to get out of the pattern of depressive thoughts?

There is an amazingly simple technique to calm the mind. It is easy go get out of any habitual thinking pattern. You only need to be a little alert and catch yourself early when you find your mind running that old damaged record. You can easily control your thinking. Only most people are not aware of the technique. There is an easy three step method to control your mind. This technique makes you a master of your thoughts. It will enable you to stop thinking and lower your brainwaves to engender a calm and relaxed state.

### Step 1: Awareness

The first step to changing anything is becoming aware that it is happening. It is also true about your thoughts. Suppose you notice your mind running a chain of thoughts that makes you sad, depressed or unhappy, or producing painful sensations in your body. The clue is not to get frustrated when you notice this. Do not try to stop those thoughts forcefully. That way you will only succeed in generating more unhappy thoughts. Why? Because, whatever you focus on expands.

The more frustrated or unhappy you get, the more you are focusing on thoughts of worry, frustration or unhappiness; so you will get more and more thoughts of frustration, worry or unhappiness. So what do you do? Simply become aware of the fact that you are thinking. Simply become aware of the fact that you are feeling unhappy. You need to do nothing more than that.

As you notice that you are thinking and feeling unhappy, smile to yourself, and take a deep breath, saying, "I just noticed myself thinking, and feeling unhappy.." When you can do just this, you will notice something very profound! If 'you' noticed 'yourself' thinking, or feeling unhappy, are there two completely different entities within you running the show of your life? You will find that there *are* these two selves within you. You will find the 'you' that notices or observes; and you will also notice that there is that 'you', which thinks unhappy thoughts and feels unhappy. The 'you' that observes the thinking entity is definitely higher than the thinking entity, just like the position of a supervisor is a higher position than the position of a worker in a factory.

So, your 'I' that observes the thoughts of unhappiness is a higher being than that which produces the thought. This higher being is the real you, the conscious being, the choice maker. Mind is the lower being, an instrument, really, which, if left to itself to run the show, will run it in an endless cycle till it reaches the edge of insanity.

The moment you become aware of the higher aspect of you as the witnessing being, you have won the first round. You are no more a slave to your mind. As you become aware, do nothing but begin to breathe slowly and deeply and notice how it feels to be present to who you really are; not the crazy mind, but you, the silent observer. Notice that there is a great feeling of peace behind that presence, the silent witness, the real you. You become aware of your power of choice making. You know that you have the power to channel your attention elsewhere, bring in some other thoughts, some positive affirmations, or you can deliberately bring some fond memories from the past, to simply replace those thoughts. Now you have the power and freedom of choice and this brings us to the step 2 of this process.

## *Step 2: Relaxed Focus*

Whatever you focus on expands. Now that you have become aware of your thinking, all you need to do is direct your attention into some other place, a place that will bring you into a state of profound relaxation. Most people do not know what that direction is.

Your conscious or objective mind thinks the thoughts that harass you. To stop those thoughts, you need to take the fuel out from your conscious mind, so that it is impotent to produce thoughts. What is this fuel that helps the conscious mind produce thoughts? You might wonder. Your own attention is that fuel. Ordinarily our attention is fully focused on and absorbed by the activities of our conscious mind. So, to deactivate the conscious mind temporarily, we need to divert the energy of attention elsewhere. To do that we need to focus on anything our body does or feels subconsciously, because, we want to bring our focus onto an activity which is beyond the grasp of our conscious, objective mind. Our breathing is such an activity, which the body goes on performing subconsciously, even when we are fast asleep. Breathing just happens without our conscious mind doing anything about it. So, our breathing can be used as an ideal object to divert and hold on our attention. Using breathing as an object of focus, we begin to feel progressively more relaxed.

What happens when you focus on your breaths? Since breathing falls in the domain of your subconscious mind, when you direct your attention to your breathing, your attention expands in the direction of this subconscious activity and your conscious thinking naturally diminishes, in the absence of the fuel. It is that simple.

Though we took a while to explain the whole process, you need not think over it, when you try to calm your mind. It is really as simple as putting on or off a switch. Just focus on your breathing and observe how your breathing is going on. Is it rapid or slow? Is it long or short? Is it rugged or smooth? Continue to do so. This brings us to Step 3.

### Step 3: Count your breath

Now begin to count your breaths. Take a deep breath in. Hold it for a short while, and slowly exhale. Count '1' for this one cycle of inhalation and exhalation. Breathe in again, hold it shortly and then exhale and count '2'. From the third breath onwards, breathe naturally, following your normal rhythm, but still maintain the count.

You may find it challenging to hold your focus in the beginning. In fact, you may be surprised to find yourself being distracted before you make it to "10" the first time. It is, because your conscious mind, the ever-thinking, thinking-machine will interrupt and distract. You may find yourself back in to the cave of mind being bombarded by a barrage of random thoughts once again. If this happens, just become aware, and begin focusing on your breathing again. Soon your mind will give up, and when you get to '20' or '25' breaths, you will begin to feel a wave of relaxation. Your thoughts will drop off on its own accord and your mind will shift from the high-frequency Beta brainwaves to a low frequency Alpha waves characterized by restful and focused awareness. This is an extremely desirable and peaceful state to abide in, and you will like to be there for a while. You may use this technique, whenever you feel your mind crowded with thoughts and whenever you need to be still.

## What thoughts should be cultivated for our happiness?

The mind is like a tape-recorder or a CD-player which is constantly running and playing whatever it likes, without caring for our permission. We should learn to consciously cultivate some positive emotions for the sake of our own happiness. We need to culture the thoughts of gratitude, forgiveness, patience, generosity and contentment. It is because, these types of thoughts creates happy waves in the mind that allows us to smile like the laughing Buddha.

The most important understanding behind this practice is that, we practice these virtues not for the sake of others, but for the sake of our own happiness. We practice them not only towards other but also towards ourselves. If you cannot forgive yourself, you cannot forgive others. If you do not have respect for yourself, you cannot possibly treat others with respect. If you are not generous to yourself, you cannot be generous to others. The Buddha taught us to practice these qualities for all fellow beings including ourselves.

# Chapter Five

## Practices for Euphoric Living

Mind is mechanical in nature and it brings forth many unwanted thoughts that might be self-destructive in nature. The mind is also vulnerable to suggestions from the world outside. Suggestions come from the friends, relatives or the mass media. These suggestions, sometimes happens to be negative in nature. The mind readily accepts them in unawareness, embraces them as its own, and believes them to be true, to its own detriment.

Allowing thoughts to pass through our mind, without some degree of vigilance, thus, can prove to be dangerous. Just as we reflect before you speak, write or act, so we should also be cautious about the ideas that enter our mind. Random negative thoughts can harm us without limit.

It is for this reason that the Buddha said, "Your worst enemy can not harm you as much as your own thoughts, unguarded. But once mastered, no one can help you as much, not even your father or your mother" (Dhammapada 3/10-11)

It is for this reason, precisely, that we should consciously practice and cultivate some thoughts and emotions that are positive and wholesome in nature.

## Thoughts Create our Destiny

Thoughts are tiny energy pockets in consciousness that wait to be manifested in reality as actions, things, people and situations. Physics has proved long before that energy cannot be destroyed in this universe. They can be transformed at the best. There is no exception to this natural law also in the domain of our thought energy. Like any other form of energy in Nature, it can bring good or bad, wanted or unwanted outcomes within our body, mind and environment, depending on how wisely or unwisely we harness it.

Thoughts are the blueprint of the movie of life. The energy of consciousness, when focused on a thought, makes it a perception in reality. A thought, cherished for a long time with enough intensity of focus, manifests as the reality by the energy of consciousness. When a thought or idea recurs repeatedly, it forms a habitual pattern and this pattern is called a conditioning. Our mind becomes conditioned to think, act or behave in a certain manner. When through conditioning, a habitual pattern of thought is established, we unconsciously believe it to be an unalterable, absolute truth. When you believe a thought to be a truth, you behave accordingly. Thoughts, thus, form a habit, habits form action, which manifest as a situation, or a series of situations. This ultimately comes to be believed as the destiny.

Most of the time people are not even aware of creating an unwanted outcome or a situation by weaving an unwholesome thought in their mind. It is also worth knowing that in the realm of thoughts, like attracts like. A thought of worry, fear or lack will attract many thoughts of the similar nature, strengthening your negative attitude, bringing the experience of misery. Similarly, a thought of joy, love, gratitude, generosity or abundance will attract similar thoughts from the cosmic repository, strengthening our own thoughts of similar kind, to manifest as good fortune.

## The Joyful Choice-Maker

Life is a miracle. We, all of us, are creator beings. We are the joyful choice-makers when we know that it is our own thoughts that matter most. Life can be viewed as a cocktail of joy and sorrow that we are forced to drink; or, we can view the life as a wonder that can be created every moment we live. It is all a matter of individual perspective. An adjustment in your focus can alter your life forever. We can live as conscious choice makers creating our life every moment of our existence.

Then why are the majority of us living their lives woven around hurt, anger, hatred, stress, tension and recrimination? It is because, people do not understand and accept the fact that by changing our own thought patterns, perception and lifestyle, we can contribute towards changing the world around us. It is, because, people fail to take responsibility of their own lives.

Buddha taught us that when we live mindfully, life can be a miracle and we can live a balanced and happy life. "When you realize how perfect everything is, you will tilt your head back and laugh at the sky." He said.

There is an abundance of positive energy within and around us, waiting to be harnessed. We all have deep wellsprings of creativity eager to find an expression. Life is a wonderful piece of art. Be creative, as much as you can, in creating it. Our own attention is the essence with which we create. Approach the life with a fresh perspective. It is your life. You have the freedom to create it, decorate it with love, compassion, joy and laughter, or mar it with brooding, blaming, anger and hatred.

## Practice of Gratitude to Attract Abundance and Happiness

The Buddha said, "More valuable than treasures in a storehouse are the treasures of the body. The most valuable of all, are the treasures of the heart." Gratitude is one of the most valuable treasures of the heart. Gratitude is essential to attract abundance in our lives. Gratitude is necessary, because, the whole universe is an interconnected web of interdependence. Every atom of this universe is somehow connected with the other. Our existence is really a shared existence.

Even in the gross physical world, every moment of our being, we are receiving from this universe. Every breath of us is borrowed from the atmosphere, from the trees that recycle the carbon dioxide to the life-giving oxygen. All the food we take in is borrowed from the earth, from the plants and animals on the planet. We could not survive, if the Sun would not caress us with warmth and energy. What would we have to drink if the rivers and streams would not provide us with pure water?

The artificial life in the city has taught human being to be so arrogant and ungrateful, that we completely forget about our dependent existence. We forget that, we survive by being on the receiving end, every moment of our life. We have forgotten to be grateful. How much grateful we are to the person who gives or lends us something we need? Our entire existence as a human being is a borrowed existence. Should we not become eternally grateful to the Sun, the earth, the plants, animals, rivers and other human beings on the planet who made our existence possible? To live with a grateful heart is the way of conscious and enlightened living.

Gratitude should be the essential norm and ethics of our life. It can change our life in a profound and miraculous way. Meister Eckhart, a German mystic used to say, "If the only prayer you say in your whole life is, 'Thank you,' that would suffice".

We should be grateful for every gift that life presents to us. There are many moments of innocent joys of living. Lord Buddha taught us the way to live mindfully. When we live mindfully, we feel grateful for those moments. We learn to be grateful for small things, like, a well-cooked bowl of food served with love and care, for an understanding co-worker, for a loving friend or relative. We learn to be grateful for all the generous and good people in our lives.

It is not necessary that gratitude needs to always express itself in a loud or pronounced utterance of thankfulness. No. It may flow as a silent under-current, as a deep feeling that fills and overflows the heart, as an emotion that humbly wraps our being with its aura of blessedness.

## Practice of Forgiveness for Freedom

There is a famous saying in the Dhammapada, the most concise and comprehensive collection of Lord Buddha's teachings. It says: 'Look how he abused me and beat me, how he threw me down and robbed me. Live with such thoughts and you live in hate. Abandon such thoughts and you live in love.' When you live in hatred you can never be truly happy, because hatred is a fire that burns your heart. Forgiveness lightens and soothes the heart by releasing you from the chain of anguish and anger.

Mind has a tendency to hold on to the memory of past hurt. By releasing the past, you walk towards a new beginning, opening the doors for better things to happen to you. This way, you are not doing a favor to others; rather you are doing favor to yourself by stepping out of the chain of suffering.

Holding on to any hurtful feelings does more damage to you than it does to anyone else. We should consciously release the hurtful baggage of the past. Know that, it is our choice to carry on the baggage or put it down forever.

By forgiving or letting go, huge amount of energy blocked as anger, hatred or revengeful thoughts is released to flow in the body, to heal the body and brighten up the mind. This creates happiness. We need to practice forgiveness to unburden ourselves and experience freedom and lightness.

## Practice of Patience and Reticence in Speech for Serenity

Patience is the golden rule for an alert and peaceful life. It brings serenity within us. It can turn every situation in our favor. Patience gives us clarity and peace. Patience makes room for making the right choice, at the right moment. In certain situations in life, it is better to wait and see rather than rushing with thoughtless speech and hasty action. If you wait for a moment before opening your mouth, you will have fewer occasions to regret what you said. Patience is the cornerstone for building a good relationship in the home and in the workplace.

The Buddha said, "Misfortune comes from one's mouth and ruins one, but fortune comes from one's heart and makes one worthy of respect." We can be happy only when we are compassionate and speak mindfully. Here is what the Buddha said about it. "Better than a thousand hollow words, is one word that brings peace." And, "The tongue is like a sharp knife...It kills without drawing blood." Hence, whatever words we utter should be chosen with care.

We should be careful enough, while using the instrument of speech. Because it can mar a relationship, as it can build a beautiful one. We would do better to remind ourselves often not to speak harshly to any one; because, angry speech is painful and it never brings peace. Both the speaker and the listener are hurt by exchange of angry words. The noble practice of patience and reticence in speech can bring much serenity in our lives and clarity in our mind.

## Practice of Generosity for Contentment

The euphoric state of the laughing Buddha reminds us to be generous and contented. Generosity illumines the heart. The word generosity can be used to mean kindness, open-heartedness, charity and bounty. Here we are using the word in every possible sense of the term. Try to be generous to someone and notice how you feel inside yourself. Every time we are generous, unfailingly we feel good, because, generosity opens the heart centre. Generosity also attracts abundance. We are here on earth to love and care, to give and share. A stingy person can never be truly happy; can never find real joy and fulfillment in life. We should make it a habit to share with others what we have.

When we practice thoughts of generosity, we automatically feel contented. We feel contented when we love and care, give and share. Contentment is a mental state of richness as discontent is a state of lack. Richness attracts more riches and lack attracts lack; this is the unfailing law of this universe. Hence, contentment is a high-energy state that automatically attracts abundance and happiness.

## Practical lessons for joyful living, in a nutshell

1. When an external situation is perceived as psychologically unbalanced, do not jump into the situation with all your energy, in an effort to fix or heal it. Remain present with the situation, try to evaluate and understand the situation and take constructive steps.

Maintaining your own balance is a stronger force to heal any situation.

2. When a situation is perceived to be unpleasant, and can not be readily changed, try to understand the situation, learn your lessons from it, and live the situation by just being with it. By experiencing an unpleasant situation with full awareness, without thoughts of mental resistances, the sting of the situation dissolves and your mental poise remains intact. Do not indulge in blaming. Take positive or corrective steps and cultivate a positive state of mind under all circumstances.

3. To develop the ability to remain balanced under all circumstances, take some moment everyday to become still and experience yourself. Stillness in itself is a higher energy state that establishes harmony within you and all around you. Experience yourself in stillness and focus on your breath or physical sensations to experience the calm and quiet center within you that is free from all conflicts and turmoil. Remember and feel this centre of stillness within you in every situation of life, and live your life from this still center.

4. To know what is right for you at a certain moment, watch your 'feel'. Allow the inner feeling to guide and direct your thoughts, words and actions. Pursue that which brings joy to you and which feels right. Trust yourself and be brave to follow your deepest impulses about what feels right.

5. To overcome the fear of insecurity, train your mind to accept and welcome the changes that come in your life. Change is an unalterable fact of this temporal existence. Welcoming changes means welcoming growth and improvement. Changes can be a harbinger for improvement in your life when you are conscious.

6. Living in the moment helps to accept and embrace the change. Impermanence is the sacred law of Nature. Hence living in the moment, we follow the course of Nature.

7. To be free from guilt, shame, lack of confidence or bad habits, practice self-love and accept yourself as you are. Then the change comes through self-observation.

8. To remove negative thoughts and emotions, observe your physical sensations, take deep breaths and breathe out the negative thoughts.

9. To banish unwanted habitual patterns of negative thinking, practice the three-step process of awareness, relaxed but focused attention on breath and counting your breaths.

10. Thoughts create our destiny. Culture the thoughts of gratitude, forgiveness, patience, generosity and contentment because, these types of thoughts creates happy waves in the mind that allows us to smile like the laughing Buddha.

# Chapter Six

## A List of To-Dos for Euphoric Living

Do everything you can, to live happily. Just use your discretion and awareness in choosing your source of bliss. You have to be alert that the joy of the present moment should not adversely affect the body and mind in the future. If the present moment of joy brings bodily and mental suffering in the future, then the joy is not wholesome in nature and it is not worth having.

All of us are allotted with a limited span of time in this human body. The time will be over, anyway, whether you choose to live it brooding, fretting and fuming, or you choose to take on the life on your terms by resolving to remain blissful, come what may. However daunting the circumstances may be, refuse to succumb before it. Learn to ignore it and remain blissful with whatever, you find, makes you happy.

When we are blissful, our luminous Self-nature peeps through the curtain of this inert physical body. This is the reason, why a blissful countenance attracts people. A blissful consciousness is ever aligned with its essence; hence, it attracts abundance, fortune and all good things on earth. When you are blissful, you emit energy of very sublime nature that never goes with darkness, disharmony, misfortune, disease, sadness or poverty. All these things will go away from you. This one practice can evolve you beyond your imagination.

Life is a work of art. Every work of art is an imagination. Imagine it beautifully, with alertness, joy and peacefulness. Every moment is our creation. We should create it afresh with joy, love, forgiveness, gratitude and wonder. If we do something to convince others, if we do something to earn a living, it does not remain an art; it becomes a business. Do it in such a way, if you must, but do at least one thing in your life in a spirit of total freedom and joy. It will unravel the hidden spring of bliss within you.

When you are expecting appreciation from people, when you want to convince others, you are really selling yourself for that appreciation. Enjoy your creation and have joy with your own uniqueness. Whatever you are doing, know that, you are creating it with your own essence, the essence of love, the essence of bliss. You are expressing yourself. Do everything in the spirit of ease and effortlessness. There is nothing to achieve. There is nobody to convince. Enjoy your work. Enjoy your creation. Enjoy your life.

Whatever you do, do it for your joy. Do it with loving attention, in an unhurried manner. The attitude of selling yourself is one of the main causes of misery. Every expectation is a selling. Whatever you do, ask yourself: "Am I feeling happy doing this?" If your answer is in negative, seriously consider changing your job or course of action.

Remember, by taking action to be happy, by remembering to be happy, you really become happy. When you become truly happy, you also become loving and generous. Your laugh and relaxation is as important for the good of the world as it is for you. A laughing Buddha does more good to the world than any somber-faced social worker. A warm heart and a clear head is the key to the smile in the face of the Laughing Buddha.

Here is a checklist for you of the to-dos for being able to live like a laughing Buddha.

## Go out in the Sun

Can Sunshine make you warm hearted? There are evidences that it can. Few know about the power of the Sunshine to elevate our mood. Like plants, we too need light to survive. Light deprivation affects us physiologically and psychologically. Light feeds not only our physical body but our mind, vital sheath and spirit as well.

It is no secret that a sunny weather induces feelings of happiness, well-being and good health. Rise in temperature was found to be in proportion with the lift in spirit. Sunny weather is also found to reduce the feelings of anxiety, depression and skepticism. The positive effects of sun on human emotions can be attributed to a neuro-chemical called Serotonin. The level of serotonin increases in sunny weather which has a positive impact on our mind. Low serotonin levels contribute to depression, sleep problems, and overeating. An important way to naturally increase serotonin is getting enough sunlight.

In the dull, dreary winters, the levels of serotonin falls and people start feeling gloomy. The sensitivity of the eyes to the sunlight also plays a part in the elevation of the mood in sunlight. Right behind our forehead there is a gland, named Pineal gland. This region is believed to be the seat of our intuition, awareness and will, and it affects our feeling of overall wellbeing and spiritual connectedness. It plays a vital role in determining the biological rhythm of the body. The Pineal gland works in harmony with the Hypothalamus gland, which directs the body's thirst, hunger, sexual desire and the biological clock that determines our aging process. Weakening of the Pineal gland hinders the brain's function, impairs our sense of direction, causes sleep disturbances and daytime tiredness. Our Pineal gland is photo-sensitive and it is a great absorber of Sunlight. A ten to twenty minutes exposure to Sunlight can stimulate and strengthen the Pineal gland.

So, make it a habit to take the Sunlight, especially in the early morning, if you can. You may not necessarily take the direct exposure, though. Working or taking your breakfast in a sunlit room or terrace is enough. Or if you can have a morning walk in a sunlit pathway, that is also great. It will boost your immune system, lift up your mood and literally light up your day. Gazing at the morning Sun for a few seconds, even as little as for one second, is also very helpful for uplifting your mood and spirit. This minimal daily dose of Sunlight will help to activate your Pineal gland, which is believed as the secret spiritual storehouse of all blessings. However, too much exposure to direct Sunlight should be avoided.

## Get enough sleep and Exercise

Good sleep and daily exercises are vital for keeping yourself in an upbeat mood and retaining the smile in your lips. Sleep deprivation increases the stress hormone, cortisol, in your body. Here it must be mentioned that more sleep does not necessarily provide you with more energy. Sleeping longer than you usually do may even put your body temperature rhythm out of balance. So you need to know just how much sleep is enough for you. You yourself are the best judge for that. Listen to your body to know just how much sleep is sufficient for you.

A daily habit to have some exercises can do a lot of good to you. You need not always go to the gym for that. Choose something, preferably some Yoga postures that suit you. As little as ten minutes of practice is enough, if you can do them regularly. If you are a beginner you need not start practicing too many Yoga postures. Select three or four postures that you can do comfortably and fit in your routine. You can have the benefit, doing as little as that. Recent studies have found that people who exercise regularly are not just more physically fit than those who do not; they are generally happier and less stressed, too. Exercise increases blood flow to your brain, counteracts the stress hormones Cortisol and Adrenaline, and releases neuro-chemicals called Endorphins in your brain, which are the 'feel-good-hormones'. The result is that you will be calmer, relaxed, and as a result, you will sleep better.

## Have a long stroll in the nature

Whether it is a ten-minute morning walk or a weekend trip to a beautiful, secluded place, spending some quiet time in a natural setting makes us our life uncluttered by making room for rest, relaxation and rejuvenation. It helps to slow down the hectic pace of life. Having a long stroll, preferably in a natural setting like a park, beach, beside a lake or river, or even in your own garden can relax you beyond measure. Do it often, if possible, everyday, and more particularly at times when you feel stressed. When you walk without a specific purpose, and you are just mindful of the sensation of the breeze at your cheeks, the sensation of your feet touching the earth, sensation of your breathing or you just enjoy the natural scenery, your tensions and anxieties automatically drops of. You live in the moment happily. Sometimes try walking barefoot on the grass. You'll have to do it yourself to feel the wonderful relaxation it brings. Even if you are busy, find out time once in a while for the outdoor activities you love.

## Take time to be still, sitting silently, feeling yourself

Everyday allot a time for yourself, even as little as ten minutes, to be alone with the most important person in your life, You. Do nothing. Just sit silently in your terrace or room. Close your eyes and feel your breathing. While you breathe out, put your attention on the feelings and sensations inside your body. Begin from your toes and then move to your ankles, calf muscles, to the upper parts of your body, and ultimately to your face and head. Do not exclude any limb. Feel your entire body as a whole. Feel your breath. Observe the breath moving in and out of your nostrils. You will notice that your breathing is becoming smoother and calmer. Feel the peace of just sitting and breathing there without having to do anything.

## Stop often to breathe deeply

Just like you take tea or coffee break right in the midst of your work, take breathing breaks! Drop for a moment everything you were doing and stop to breathe deeply. It will relax you immediately, and much tension will drop away, as a result. You will feel calmer, more focused and clear-headed. Your efficiency too will increase as a result.

## Practice self care and self-love

Learn to love yourself. In the entire world there is nobody, no body exactly like you. There has never been another person like you, since the beginning of time. Nobody has your eyes, your glance, your smile, your handwriting or your voice. Each of us is a unique creation of the Divine and we need to admire ourselves for that. Love yourself not for the things you have done or plan to do, but love yourself for who you are. Love your uniqueness, your personality, your character traits and everything else that makes you who you are. The more you love yourself, the stronger and more positive you will feel about your life. Make it a conscious practice, a regular, daily discipline, to care for you and acknowledge the strong points about you.

People often have the perception that self-love will happen naturally once they change something about them (like losing weight or achieving a goal). It is a wrong way of thinking, which seldom works. Self-love has to come first. Self love is an important ingredient for happiness.

All people, even all beings, regardless of their gender, capacity or social standing, inherently possess the Buddha nature, the quality of a Buddha. Hence, all beings, including we ourselves are equally worthy of our love and respect. "You can search throughout the entire universe for someone who is more deserving of your love and affection than you are yourself, and that person is not to be found anywhere. You yourself, as much as anybody in the entire universe deserve your love and affection." The Buddha said.

Take good care of yourself. You are as deserving of your attention as anybody else is. Your world begins with your body. Take care of your body. Do everything to keep it pure, fresh, fit and free from diseases. The Buddha used to urge his disciples to take care of them. "Your body is precious. It is your vehicle for awakening. Treat it with care." He used to say. And here is his recipe for physical and mental health. "The secret of health for both the mind and the body is not to mourn for the past, nor to worry about the future, but to live the present moment wisely and earnestly."

Positive affirmations and visualizations may play an important role to enhance self-love. Positive affirmations can change your thinking patterns as they have profound effect on the subconscious mind.

Visualize good performances, success, and positive outcomes for all your efforts. Your self-image, that is, how you see yourself, is also important. Visualize yourself in a positive way, as intelligent, caring, and brave, for example. Do not dwell on your flaws. Positive visualization encourages the release of "feel good hormones" called Endorphins. There is an interesting principle behind it. The body does not know the difference between something that you are only visualizing versus something that you are actually experiencing. This was proven when Olympic athletes were connected to EKG machines and imagined running through their athletic performance with their eyes closed. The exact same muscles fired as when they actually performed their event. If the muscles can fire only by visualizing the body running and moving, then imagine the world of good we can do to ourselves by regularly visualizing a positive self-image.

**A special lesson of self-care at difficult times:**

Unfortunately, difficult times can make us feel unworthy and somewhat forgotten by the world (or even forgotten by the heaven). Ironically, this can lead us to treat ourselves unkindly at a time when what we really need is to support ourselves. We must watch out for this. And if life has, for the moment, failed to recognize our value and our needs, we must not fail to do so. Remember that our life-lessons and circumstances are never meant to call into question our value and our worthiness, as some religions wrongly teach. Though circumstances may challenge us, our lessons are never sent to punish us. We are just as worthy, just as whole, just as loved by the Divine, on the rough roads as on the smooth. During difficult times, our power lies in remembering this and practicing it in our lives. When we do that, the extra self-imposed burden and pressure will magically lift away from us. And the heaven will smile too.

# Have a shift in attitude: Shift from surviving to really living

Life is not something you just get along with. Life is not something to spend casually and carelessly. Life is precious and you are here because you chose to be here. Knowing this you can not but be more mindful in living your life. From surviving to really living, this shift in attitude will add a new dimension to your life. Add a personal flavor to everything you do. Find new ways to do the ordinary things of life. Add uniqueness to everything you do. Remember that you are unique in this entire creation and everything you do, say or create carries your signature of uniqueness. Respect the uniqueness of everything in this creation as you respect your own uniqueness. Live every moment of your life with a zest, intensity and a purpose. Never allow yourself to just drag on. Know what you are doing, and why you are doing what you are doing.

## Simplify your living

Keeping things simple in life is an extraordinary feat that you should endeavor to attain for a happy living. It should be applied in every aspect of life. Do not stuff your life with an awful number of things, gadgets, social appointments and jobs to be done. Getting rid of the unnecessary things will tremendously help you to find peace and calm in your everyday life. You will be a lot happier and calmer when you live a clutter-free life.

One of the biggest blockages to happiness comes from too much stuff in your life, whether these are material things or activities. Having more is not always better. In today's world consumerism is contagious and it is a hard habit to break. People often equate 'things' with happiness. But it is mere common sense that a life-long pursuit of more and more things only leads to less happiness. Consumerism makes you believe that you can not 'live' without a certain thing; in most cases, this is a false belief. If you closely examine, you will find that you really need a few things to live, and live happily. Working sixty hours a week to pay for things you do not really need makes your life complicated, leaves you stressful and in the process, there is little space left for really enjoying life.

Each one of us is allotted a certain span of life. Make use of it in a way that is really meaningful. Simplifying your life is a great step to live a meaningful, happy life. De-clutter your life to make room for happiness. Even physical clutters can add visual stress and frustration to our lives. Most people will agree that walking into a tidy room, whether it is the kitchen, living room, office or bedroom, puts their minds into a more peaceful state. When the space is clean, free of clutters, maintaining it in its clean state is much simpler. The things you have not used in a year or two may well make their way to your list of things to get rid of. You will find that letting go of stuffs you do not really need is very enlightening as well as unburdening. You will find that, in this sense, less is more. Getting rid of unnecessary things brings more peace, calm and clarity. Space is beautiful. Have more space in your life!

Another step to a simpler living is the ability to leave your work at your place of work. Work is work and home is home. Being able to maintain this will help to make your life less stressful.

## Appreciate the beauty of life in trivia

Remind yourself often to take life less seriously. We should learn to appreciate the inherent beauty of life that peeps as much through the graceful smile of a wrinkled old face as through the innocent smile of a baby. Everywhere and in everything the beauty and wonder of Life is peeping through. As we grow old, we forget to get in touch with that. We forget to appreciate the beauty hidden in a piece of rock or a lump of clay, with which a child may play for hours. The mind needs to be consciously trained to reclaim the lost paradise of the childhood, to learn to wonder just about anything.

You can do that by consciously paying attention to the little joys of having a healthy body, being able to breathe the fresh air, walking on the grass, having a cup of tea, relaxing and enjoying a soothing music and the like. These little joys are very easily available to most of us but our minds are normally trained to be neutral to these experiences or simply ignore them. We are often caught in the habit of taking things and people for granted. That is a sure recipe for living an insipid, joyless life.

The mind remains caught in the net of thinking, and takes note of these so called 'trivial' experiences, only when there is a lack. For example, we are aware of what a blessings a healthy body is, when we are sick. We are aware of the bliss that breathing offers only when we have caught cold and have a blocked nose. Thus, the normal, unconscious training of the mind is only to take note of the lacks. It is understandable why boredom and unhappiness is so widespread, even among those that have apparently everything required for a happy living.

For living our life to the fullest, we need to teach our minds to enjoy small things. From time to time remind yourself to have a notice of the small things happening around you and amuse yourself with that. Remind yourself often not to take life too seriously. Sincerity and seriousness is not the same thing. Sincerity adds integrity and dignity to our character, while too much seriousness robs us of the ability to laugh, enjoy and smile at the funny side of life.

Learn to laugh and giggle. We may learn from the children. They have the unique gift of spontaneously living in the moment and having fun in just about any situation. Form a habit to see beauty and wonder in everything and everybody, including you. This habit will completely wipe away the negative conditionings of the past and make your life full of joy.

Enjoy making fun about yourself. You can do this by sometimes describing you in the third person, replacing the nagging "I" with 'he' or 'she', when you catch yourself doing or saying something funny or irrational. You can play this game with a close friend. Try it and you will find this game of describing yourself in the third person very absorbing and enlightening. You can do this when you learn to love and accept yourself totally as you are. This will help you learn to accept your fellow beings as they are, and not as they should be, according to your mental interpretations. You learn to accept and enjoy life as it unfolds, and do not impose conditions on it. For this, you need to take time to be quiet and to appreciate the beauty of life.

Goal oriented persons are seldom happy in life. They set one goal after another and with their mind set only on the goal, they often forget to enjoy what life offers on the way, and in the process miss the life totally. Learn to enjoy the way as much as you would enjoy when you reach the destination. We should never take life too seriously. Life is a play and we should play it spiritedly.

### Everyday find at least one reason to be grateful

Life brings so many blessings to us every day. A loving, caring and loyal friend is a blessing. An understanding and loving spouse is a blessing. A considerate colleague is a blessing. A warm smile from a stranger is a blessing. A healthy body is a blessing. A beautiful sunset is a blessing. The warm sunlit morning is a blessing. The peaceful morning breeze on your cheek is a blessing. You can go on and on like this. The number is more than you can count.

But how many of us live mindful of these blessings? There are many who live totally forgetful of these blessings that life offers to them, for free! And they grumble that they have little reason to be grateful to life. Such people are unworthy of having a blissful life.

Make a habit to find at least one reason everyday to be grateful to life. It will enrich your life beyond your imagination. When you awaken to the blessings of your life, more and more blessings pour in, and you start living a euphoric life.

## Do something to make someone, anyone happy. Be nice.

Being nice is the easiest and most affordable gift you can bring to others as well as to yourself. You do not need to spend a penny for that. Niceness is never overrated. People who are not nice create lots of unnecessary misery for themselves and others. Niceness, on the other hand, creates tons of joy. Be kind to someone. Be generous. Praise someone, anyone. Many flowers of Joy will blossom in the tree of your life to make you really feel euphoric.

## Relax, breathe, listen to music or do something you love.

People keep themselves busy in their life to keep appointments, to take care of their jobs and often to care for their spouse, children or aged parents. While to live for others is admirable, it seldom makes you happy, if in the process you totally forget to take care of yourself. When you neglect to take care of yourself day after day, ultimately tiredness, mental fatigue and boredom takes over you, leaving you operating on the lowest level of your efficiency. It will make you edgy and easily irritable.

To be able to contribute to the world and to the life of your near and dear ones calmly and consistently over a long period of time, you need to take good care of yourself. It is necessary to take time to relax, breathe, listen to some uplifting music or do something you really love to do. Create a special time for yourself, an appointment with yourself. Just relax, breathe and be with yourself. You may make use of aromatherapy, listen to soothing music or do anything you love. Remember that joy is inherent in our nature. When you take time to spend with yourself, learn to relax, stop to breathe and do what you love, you are bestowing these are gifts to yourself that will open up the hidden source of joy within you.

## Smile often and laugh wholeheartedly at least once a day.

A smile can create happiness in the home, foster goodwill in the business and has the power to create a friendship. A smile costs you nothing but gives back much in return. It enriches those who receive, without making you poorer while you give it away. It takes but a moment but creates a memory that sometimes lasts forever. Your smile has tremendous value. It can bring rest to the weary heart, cheer and sunshine to the one that is sad and discouraged. Those that are too tired to give a smile are really pitiable. Both laughter and smiling are contagious. When you smile at someone they usually reciprocate with a smile. This establishes a connection between people. An authentic smile and a sincere laughter can make one's day brighter. Moreover, the simple act of smiling and laughter release Endorphins, the 'feel-good chemicals' in the brain. It lowers the stress hormones and strengthens the immune system. Remind yourself to smile often, and laugh or giggle wholeheartedly at least once in a day. A simple belly laugh in the style of laughing Buddha has much therapeutic effect apart from its power to light up your day. Try it and see the result for yourself.

## Live mindfully

Living mindfully is an indispensable condition for euphoric living. When you live being lost in the net of thoughts and worries and fantasies, you do not truly live. You just manage to survive. To live life to the fullest, you have to live mindfully. You have to be present in whatever you do. Eat mindfully. Have a shower mindfully. Walk mindfully. Talk, listen, breathe and walk mindfully. If you live this way, your whole life will be lighted with the light of self-awareness; it will be a beauty to look at, perceive, and savor.

Begin from being mindful when you eat. The adage that you are what you eat, is not without its merit. Proper food is crucial, among other things, for self-growth and happiness. Foods are important because they make your blood, cell, bones and muscles of your body and influence your thoughts and emotions. Food grown organically and prepared with care, attention and love are rich in vital energies. They are capable of raising your vital energy and vibrations, just as a piece of good music or spending time with the Nature can. Hence, food needs to be savored, rather than gulped down the throat, as if it is just another chore you have to get over with. Shift your awareness to the food in your mouth, and focus on taste, texture, flavor and aroma. You will obtain much more than just the nutrients from the food you eat. You will absorb the vital energies within it more fully.

Next watch yourself, your postures, your style of talking, and your breathing. Watch how you sit, stand and interact with people. Watch your thoughts and emotions. Remove negative thoughts like you remove the weeds from your garden. Self-awareness is another name of self-love. Falling in love with yourself is most crucial for euphoric living.

## Act happy and think happy thoughts

Act the way you want to feel and soon you will feel the way you act. This is a most ancient secret, though nowadays it is commonly used in self confidence building therapies or courses where you are asked to act like a confident person. You will soon develop that skill or behavior which results in more confidence in you. There is increasing evidence that acting enraged, obsessed, malevolent, or depressed may prove bad for you. This is true because, the mind can not distinguish between something you really experience and something you just act out, just like the body can not distinguish between something you really experience or just visualize with your mind. Actor Leonard DiCaprio is said to develop obsessive-compulsive disorder while playing Howard Hughes in the block buster The Aviator. This often happens to actors who get caught up in the roles they play. If you act having an enraged or angry conversation with someone, you will usually find that your emotions do get enraged even though you are simply acting the part.

This principle has powerful implication for your happiness. Your body language and thoughts have much to do with the level of happiness you experience in your life. When you are acting happy, you are thinking happy thoughts that go with acting the role you are playing. The body can not distinguish between the act and real happiness and it generates happiness-hormones, creating real waves of happiness in your mind. So try acting happy. Deliberately think happy thoughts and remember happy moments of your life. As you act happy, deliberately think happy thoughts by remembering happy moments of your life.

Just like acting happy, thinking happy thoughts also multiplies happiness in your life by the ancient law of life which decrees that whatever you focus on expands. This principle goes hand in hand with the law of momentum. What is the law of momentum? To put simply, it is: Energy in motion, tends to stay in motion and energy stopped, tends to stay stopped. In other words, this principle can be interpreted as follows. If you take action in your life to create happiness, you will experience more and more happiness every day. Happiness breeds more happiness. The law of momentum is in operation everywhere in life, in physics, within our body, and most importantly, it works even in the domain of our thoughts.

Our thinking works on the basis of the law of focus and momentum. Our mind is like a large pool of potential thinking energy, just waiting for us to give it a direction to it. It awaits and responds to every command from us. Only, most of us are not very experienced at giving command to our mind. In fact, a lot of people are not even aware that they can have a control over their thoughts. Instead they allow the mind to run in whatever direction it will naturally gravitate to, thereby creating much unhappiness and misery for them.

Your mind is a great pool of thought energy resembling a great overflowing lake that is just waiting for an outlet to pour into. When you do not give a direction to it, the water, (in this case, your thoughts) just takes the course it naturally finds. If you are habituated to think sad, depressive or negative thoughts, there is a natural channel in your mind to allow the flow of thoughts in that direction. The thought energy like the flow of water slowly trickles down in that direction. That trickle turns in to a stream in no time. The stream turns in to a small river which ultimately takes the shape of a giant, unstoppable waterfall, completely overwhelming you with its force. This is the way how our mind or thought works. This is why giving a conscious direction to our thoughts is important. This is where thinking happy thoughts come to immense help in creating a new channel and directing the pool of mind energy flow through this channel. Ultimately this small stream of happy thoughts expands to form a mighty river and even a giant waterfall of immense strength, creating mighty splashes of euphoria and ecstasy within your being.

# A Fifteen Point Checklist for Euphoric Living

1. Go out in the Sun.
2. Get enough sleep and Exercise.
3. Have a long stroll in the nature.
4. Take some time to be still, sitting silently alone, feeling yourself.
5. Stop often to breathe deeply.
6. Practice self care and self-love and be compassionate to you during difficult times.
7. Have a shift in your attitude: Shift from surviving to really living your life.
8. Simplify your living and de-clutter your house and life.
9. Appreciate the beauty of life in trivia and remind yourself often to take life less seriously
10. Everyday, find at least one reason to be grateful.
11. Do something to make someone, anyone happy. Be nice.
12. Take time to relax, breathe, listen to uplifting music or do something you love.
13. Remind yourself to smile often and laugh wholeheartedly at least once a day.
14. Live mindfully.
15. Act happy and think happy thoughts.

# Chapter Seven

## Living as Laughing Buddha Here and Now

*"I see now that all creatures have perfect enlightenment within their being - but they do not know it."* --Buddha

In the preceding paragraphs, we have discussed some practices to live a euphoric life like a living Laughing Buddha. However, when you learn more about the working of your mind, you will find that happiness has little to do with 'having' something, or 'doing' something; it is a state of your 'being', which appears when you have less or no thoughts. Happiness is our natural state of being. It gets a chance to manifest in our life when we do not block it. In ultimate essence, being the Laughing Buddha is learning not to be unhappy.

The scientists have 'discovered' that most of the things we think will make us happy, do not really make us happy, at least not for long. For example, to their surprise, they found that money, beyond enough for basic needs, does not bring more happiness. Nor do the things that money can buy. Research has shown that even people who win vast sums in a lottery, after just a few years are as miserable as they were before they won. Things and persons that once used to make you happy lose their charm in the long run, as in this world of impermanence everything gets old, wears out, or your mind simply craves for something new.

After a while, our mind take 'things', including people, for granted; even things that once made us ecstatic fail to provide satisfaction. For example, think of your new car or house, the new dress or the new technological gadget. The initial thrill soon wears away, and then you are looking for something better and newer. It is what the scientists call the 'hedonic treadmill'. We adapt to things so fast. The more possessions and accomplishments we have, the more we need to have, to keep boosting our level of happiness.

Nothing can make us happy, if we do not allow happiness to happen within our being. Since everybody is unique in their mental make-up, there is no universal recipe for happiness. What makes one happy may not bring happiness to another. For example, a rich and spicy dinner may bring happiness to someone used to such food, while it may not be even agreeable to someone used to a different food habit. If you are an artist, finishing a nice piece of painting may bring you such happiness as no material thing can offer.

Having good foods, a great job, a nice house, a nice car and a kind mate are socially accepted norms for a happy living. However, if these things would buy happiness, then the persons having these things would always be in a happy state of mind. The probability would be that the richest persons would be the happiest in the world. However, we all know that the fact is often contrary. Happiness is never a thing that money, relationship or any other material things can buy. Moreover, happiness is a very fleeting sensation, which often slips out of hand in this temporal world where everything is in constant change.

If you live with an open eye, you will seldom find a happy person. You will find persons who might have all the things to be happy, judged by material and social standards, but still be very unhappy. A loss in the share market may make someone unhappy. A stray comment from an office colleague can mar our day, making us unhappy. A remark from a neighbor may make us feel miserable. If you are at the mercy of others, things and people, to make you happy, then, happiness will elude you forever. If your happiness depends on things outside of your being, like a thing, a person or a situation, this means slavery to these external conditions. A slave seldom gets happiness. In that case, unhappiness would be a constant shadow following your happiness. To come out of this trap, we need to find happiness within ourselves, which can be permanent.

## Naturally Happy

Happiness is the natural state of our being. According to scientists, happiness is a very desirable state. The evidences show that happy people live longer than depressed people. Happy people are healthier, more resilient, and perform better than others. In one study, the difference in life span was nine years between the happiest group and the unhappiest group. So that's a huge effect.

However, the quest for happiness is a fine trick of our unconscious nature to fool us. The paradoxical thing about happiness is that it comes from within rather than from some external objects, as we usually believe. You need to understand that happiness, really, is something happening within your consciousness. It does not solely depend on the external conditions. If you spend time reflecting on the behavior of your own mind, you may be surprised by what you discover.

You will find that happiness is something that is always available. Everyone occasionally displays their natural state of happiness. A thing or a person you love makes you happy, because your attention gets absorbed in to that and this absorption silences the random dialogues in your mind, albeit momentarily. Hence, the feelings of happiness you feel. When the fresh charm of the thing or the person wears away and you take them for granted, the same thing or person looses the ability to absorb your mind. As a result, the random thoughts in your minds return and the happiness initially derived from this thing or person fades away.

The same thing is true when something you do makes you happy. It happens when you are totally absorbed in doing something you enjoy. At such moments, you are not influenced by other thoughts. This could be anything from gardening, being engaged in some adventure sports, going for trekking, listening to a good piece of music, speaking to a friend on the phone, playing an instrument or any other fulfilling activity. Have you ever noticed how you feel at such moments of absorption? What does it feel like when you are absorbed or engaged in an activity? You feel happy. There is no doubt about this.

Your mind needs to do nothing for you to be happy. It just needs to be absorbed in some enjoyable activity so that it does not produce random thoughts. Again, if you do the same thing for long, it may no longer interest you and your happiness disappears leaving a sense of boredom. For example take the example of gardening. You love doing it and you are happy when you do that. However, if the same job becomes a compulsion for you, the charm quickly disappears, leaving a sense of drudgery. So, happiness has little to do with 'having' something, or 'doing' something; it is a state of your 'being', which appears when you have less or no thoughts.

Think what happens when you become angry or upset for some reason. Your mind produces a flurry of thoughts. When you are emotionally challenged, your mind continuously churns out thoughts of negative nature and it is violently engaged in this activity. When we are angry, resentful, anxious, or depressed, the conscious or ego-mind is totally active in producing a flood of thoughts. We can not experience these emotions without thoughts surging through our mind. Also think what happens when you are bored. Your mind is engaged in producing random thoughts. A torrent of thoughts in our consciousness blocks the natural flow of happiness within us. And if these thoughts are of unhappy nature, we become miserable.

From this it follows that it is the thoughts that make you feel unhappy or bored, whereas real happiness is a state of no thoughts. So, unhappiness or boredom can be 'created', by thoughts. Happiness, on the contrary, can not be created. It manifests itself naturally and spontaneously as the thoughts are removed, when the mind is absorbed in something, a person or in an engaging activity.

These observations give us some insight about happiness. We do not need mind, aka the thought producing machine to be happy. Happiness is our natural state of being. When we are engaged in a pleasant activity, happiness flows out unconsciously. When we relax, we naturally feel happiness. When our mind is devoid of random and negative thoughts and emotions, we naturally feel happy. It just happens naturally.

Hence for a euphoric living, in the first place we need to learn not to cherish or cultivate unhappy thoughts. Next we need to learn to cultivate happy thoughts. We learn to live mindfully which stills the random dialogue of the mind, and most importantly, we need to learn to become still sometimes that unlocks the gate of happiness within. We may sometimes focus on our breathing to still random thoughts of the mind. That is all we need to do to abide in our natural state of happiness. Of course, there use to be seeds of subtle psychological irritants within us, which need to be uprooted by constant mindfulness.

## Focus on the Bliss within

When we know that happiness is readily available with us, always, when we know that we have never lost it, we can challenge ourselves to start living a happier life here and now. There is nothing wrong in finding happiness from the external objects and people, so long as you are aware of their impermanent nature, so long as you are prepared to let them go, if required, and remain happy within your own being. Loving yourself is the key to finding happiness within your being.

As your mind becomes more and more subtle, you will find it easy to tune with the inner melody of bliss that flows within like a stream buried under the sands. Keep your focus on that unborn, undying bliss. Any external cause of happiness only unravels or manifests only a part of that inner river of bliss. The key to maintain the glimpse of this inner stream of happiness is to keep your focus on the inner feeling of joy in any joyful situation of life. Be it listening to your favorite music, talking to someone you love, painting, gardening, writing, singing, or just walking, anything that keeps you absorbed.

Do what you love to do. Be where you love to be. Only thing to remember is to keep your focus on the joy that flows from within, along with the feel of the object outside. Living in this way, you will be unaffected by the changes that takes place outside in natural course with the passage of time. Gradually, you will be able to feel happiness just for no reason at all. Then you know that you do have the power within you to be blissful under all circumstances.

This life is meant to be a song of celebration. This life is meant to be a song of peace, harmony and unity. This life is meant for loving and caring, giving and sharing. This universe was created for that. In fact the word universe literally means that; 'uni' means single, or one and 'verse' means poetry or song. This whole existence is one song of unity. We are inseparably connected with all that exists. We are made of the essence called love, bliss, or presence. We came here and manifested as humans to share our essence, to have a taste of our own essence. We will be here for the whole of eternity. This life is but a brief snapshot of our eternal being. Nothing, even the death is not so powerful to rob us of the essence we are made of, which is pure bliss. Let this knowledge sink deep within you. Let it flow within you through all you think, speak and do. Let this knowledge help you to shake off all fears and gloom if they occasionally come your way. Clouds can never mask the Sun permanently. We are that Sun, the Sun of immortal love and bliss. We, each one of us deserve and can live a euphoric life every moment, being the very embodiment of the Laughing Buddha.

-:-

# About the Author:

**Sakshi Chetana** is a popular teacher of Buddhist meditation and author on mind-body-spirit meditation, Buddha lifestyle and infinite human potential. She is author of several books on Yoga and Buddhism, including "Laughing Buddha: The Alchemy of Euphoric Living" and "In Love with Yourself". She is currently writing a book "Yoga body, Buddha mind and Zen Living". She has lived in a Himalayan province in the northern India since 2006.

She can be reached at sakshichetana@gmail.com

# Also from Inner Light Publishers

## Awakening Inner Guru: The Way to Fulfilment

*Awakening Inner Guru* is a clear and straightforward guide to awaken the light within.

For those who are truly interested to attain spiritual freedom and fulfillment in every sphere of life, this book is a practical and personal manual.

ISBN: 9788191026900

## Om Chanting and Meditation

Om is our blissful Self. Om is the mysterious cosmic energy that is the substratum of all the things and all the beings. It is the eternal song of the Divine. This book makes the Om meditation easy to follow, simple to do, and very effective.

ISBN: 9788191026931

# Yoga and Meditation: Getting Connected with Eternal Bliss

This book redefines the concept of Yoga with astounding simplicity and clarity, making it compatible with modern life-style.

This is an inspiring user-friendly guidebook for navigating and living the ancient science of Yoga and Meditation as a path to joy, happiness and freedom.

ISBN: 9788191026955

We at Inner Light Publishers are dedicated to publishing books that helps improve the quality of human lives. You are welcome to visit us at www.inner-light-in.com.

Printed in Great Britain
by Amazon